Titles by *Langaa* RPCIG

Francis B. Nyamnjoh
Stories from Abakwa
Mind Searching
The Disillusioned African
The Convert
Souls Forgotten
Married But Available

Dibussi Tande
No Turning Back. Poems of Freedom 1990-1993

Kangsen Feka Wakai
Fragmented Melodies

Ntemfac Ofege
Namondo. Child of the Water Spirits
Hot Water for the Famous Seven

Emmanuel Fru Doh
Not Yet Damascus
The Fire Within
Africa's Political Wastelands: The Bastardization of Cameroon
Oriki'badan
Wading the Tide

Thomas Jing
Tale of an African Woman

Peter Wuteh Vakunta
Grassfields Stories from Cameroon
Green Rape: Poetry for the Environment
Majunga Tok: Poems in Pidgin English
Cry, My Beloved Africa
No Love Lost
Straddling The Mungo: A Book of Poems in English & French

Ba'bila Mutia
Coils of Mortal Flesh

Kehbuma Langmia
Titabet and the Takumbeng
An Evil Meal of Evil

Victor Elame Musinga
The Barn
The Tragedy of Mr. No Balance

Ngessimo Mathe Mutaka
Building Capacity: Using TEFL and African Languages as Development-oriented Literacy Tools

Milton Krieger
Cameroon's Social Democratic Front: Its History and Prospects as an Opposition Political Party, 1990-2011

Sammy Oke Akombi
The Raped Amulet
The Woman Who Ate Python
Beware the Drives: Book of Verse

Susan Nkwentie Nde
Precipice
Second Engagement

Francis B. Nyamnjoh & Richard Fonteh Akum
The Cameroon GCE Crisis: A Test of Anglophone Solidarity

Joyce Ashuntantang & Dibussi Tande
Their Champagne Party Will End! Poems in Honor of Bate Besong

Emmanuel Achu
Disturbing the Peace

Rosemary Ekosso
The House of Falling Women

Peterkins Manyong
God the Politician

George Ngwane
The Power in the Writer: Collected Essays on Culture, Democracy & Development in Africa

John Percival
The 1961 Cameroon Plebiscite: Choice or Betrayal

Albert Azeyeh
Réussite scolaire, faillite sociale : généalogie mentale de la crise de l'Afrique noire francophone

Aloysius Ajab Amin & Jean-Luc Dubois
Croissance et développement au Cameroun :
d'une croissance équilibrée à un développement équitable

Carlson Anyangwe
Imperialistic Politics in Cameroun:
Resistance & the Inception of the Restoration of the Statehood of Southern Cameroons

Bill F. Ndi
K'Cracy, Trees in the Storm and Other Poems
Map: Musings On Ars Poetica

Kathryn Toure, Therese Mungah Shalo Tchombe & Thierry Karsenti
ICT and Changing Mindsets in Education

Charles Alobwed'Epie
The Day God Blinked

G.D. Nyamndi
Babi Yar Symphony
Whether losing, Whether winning
Tussles: Collected Plays

Samuel Ebelle Kingue
Si Dieu était tout un chacun de nous?

Ignasio Malizani Jimu
Urban Appropriation and Transformation : bicycle, taxi and handcart operators in Mzuzu, Malawi

Justice Nyo' Wakai:
Under the Broken Scale of Justice: The Law and My Times

John Eyong Mengot
A Pact of Ages

Ignasio Malizani Jimu
Urban Appropriation and Transformation: Bicycle Taxi and Handcart Operators

Joyce B. Ashuntantang
Landscaping and Coloniality: The Dissemination of Cameroon Anglophone Literature

Jude Fokwang
Mediating Legitimacy: Chieftaincy and Democratisation in Two African Chiefdoms

Michael A. Yanou
Dispossession and Access to Land in South Africa: an African Perspevctive

Tikum Mbah Azonga
Cup Man and Other Stories

John Nkemngong Nkengasong
Letters to Marions (And the Coming Generations)

Amady Aly Dieng
Les étudiants africains et la littérature négro-africaine d'expression française

Tah Asongwed
Born to Rule: Autobiography of a life President

Frida Menkan Mbunda
Shadows From The Abyss

Bongasu Tanla Kishani
A Basket of Kola Nuts

Fo Angwafo III S.A.N of Mankon
Royalty and Politics: The Story of My Life

Royalty and Politics

The Story of My Life

Fo Angwafo III S.A.N of Mankon

Langaa Research & Publishing CIG
Mankon, Bamenda

Publisher:
Langaa RPCIG
(*Langaa* Research & Publishing Common Initiative Group)
P.O. Box 902 Mankon
Bamenda
North West Region
Cameroon
Langaagrp@gmail.com
www.langaapublisher.com

Distributed outside N. America by African Books Collective
orders@africanbookscollective.com
www.africanbookscollective.com

Distributed in N. America by Michigan State University Press
msupress@msu.edu
www.msupress.msu.edu

ISBN: 9956-558-31-1

© Fo Angwafo III S.A.N of Mankon 2009
First published 2009

DISCLAIMER

All views expressed in this publication are those of the author and do not necessarily reflect the views of Langaa RPCIG.

Contents

1. Growing up in Colonial times 1

2. The Big Surprise 13

3. The Plebiscite: My Initiation into Politics 21

4. Fo Mankon and Politician 29

5. SDF the Reincarnation of KNDP 33

6. Churches, Schools and Politics 47

7. Building the Palace, Tending the Kingdom 57

8. My Life in Photos 71
   - Young Prince 73
   - Fo Mankon 75
   - MaFo 95
   - Fo and Politics 99
   - Abengafo 113
   - Awards 139

1

Growing up in Colonial times

I am surprised that after about 84 years of life, I am telling the story of my life, sitting in the place where I was born. I never knew that I would come to be Fo Mankon and even die here at the palace. I was born in 1925, on May 21, right here in *Nto' Mankon*, and named Anyeghamotü. I am the son of Fo Ndefru III, who ascended to the throne in 1919 – roughly at the beginning of the British administration of the Southern Cameroons, and who died on March 31, 1959, about two years to the end of British colonial rule. My mother, Theresa Mankah, who was to become Mafo Angwafo III (Queen Mother) in 1959, was one of his wives. She was the daughter of Akenji and Swiri, both from Munki (Asongkah), one of the quarters of Mankon. I am her only surviving son, my brother, her other son, having passed away when he was barely 12 years old. My father had married over a hundred wives, and I was saddled with the responsibility of taking over them. When I succeeded my father in 1959, I took over as well 79 of his wives who were still here at the palace. I was far away from Mankon and Mezam Division when I lost my father on that fateful day. I was the main Agriculture Official sent to open the agricultural department of the now Menchum and Boyo Divisions. When we came for the sad event, least did I expect that I was not going back.

I had never thought for a moment that I could be incarnated Fon in succession to the office of Fo Mankon. My mother had an only brother who was not financially able to help her or even to extend the help to me. And so, imagine that in such a large family, though our father was interested in education, the number of wives, the number of children, the number of extended family overpowered him and so he couldn't support our school. One of his principles to us his children was for our uncles to support our schooling. I had no uncle to go to.

However, my father sent me to school – Government School Bamenda – in 1934 for the love of education, but he didn't understand education. When it came to supplying my school needs, school fees and upbringing, it was difficult. So in that 1934, I was sent to stay with our eldest brother who had been employed in 1931. On the little he earned, this brother was taking care of all of us staying with him and of himself, and he just couldn't maintain himself and couldn't help us, much as he tried. And so I began having difficulties with my education.

By 1937 I left my father to stay with my age groups in a small grass house we made for ourselves in Atua-Zire. I left the Government School Bamenda Station to meet them in the newly opened Catholic Mission School Mankon, because it was necessary for us to live together in order to fend for ourselves. We came home occasionally to collect food stuff, cook our food and fetch firewood for sale in Ntambag (town) and also for our own use. From time to time my mother would carry food and come to give me at Bamenda Station. If on Friday I didn't come home, she will come. She was a nice and caring mother, and she would cook rice, achu and other types of food, and bring to me at school. She was also a very submissive wife to my father, soft and quiet. Farming was part and parcel of my mother's life. She cultivated food crops for her household and part for the market in Ntambag. She engaged me in this task by taking me to the farm. My father, apart from being a hunter and a lover of art, was also an ardent farmer, something that would bring him a contract from the British Administration to supply food to the Bamenda prison.

It was school that took me away from the palace. There was no idea of ever renting a house to stay in. Nobody thought that renting a house was a business, and my father too, he didn't like the idea of us or any of his children ever passing nights in Ntambag, which was mostly inhabited by strangers. My father didn't like the lifestyle of the strangers and he didn't like any of us being associated with these ways. And if we went to Ntambag, we went to sell firewood and foodstuff.

The Catholic Mission School was first established here at Ntambeng in 1935. In 1936, it was transferred to Ntahsen. Some of my colleagues Bongam, Ntah and others entered that school. I left Government School Bamenda, because I was lonely there, to meet them in the Catholic Mission School. I also went there because my elder brother, Joseph Fru-Asah Ndomu, was Catholic. Whilst we were up at Government School Bamenda Station, we normally went down for catechumen in Mankon. So when in 1937 I decided to leave and to join the Catholic Mission School, I didn't know that I had angered my father who preferred the government school. Although it would appear that my father was hostile to mission education, at a closer look, nothing could be further from the truth. He did a lot for them. My father cooperated with the respective missionaries in the development of education and Christianity, by making land available and by providing labour when needed, for the building of schools and churches. Land was also generously made available for other social services, in particular, for the building of the Bamenda General Hospital.

What he didn't like was the Catholic doctrine of one man, one woman. Worst still, he loathed celibacy. He never took priests seriously because they were not married. He would call a priest and say, 'Father, come, a good man like you – no wife? How are you? When you die, who will take care of the things you leave behind? Who will succeed you?' The man would tell him he has brothers and sisters to take care of things when he is gone. My father couldn't take seriously anyone who failed to give the social responsibility of marriage the respect it deserved. He was afraid that if all of us married only one woman, this would jeopardise the institution of Kingdom. He loved the Catholics, what they envisioned – the civilizing influence of education – but when it came to the family, he disagreed with their emphasis on men marrying only one wife. That, he didn't like.

I myself did not know my father's opinion about the Catholic Church and marriage, but I enjoyed going with my age group to catechumen and for that I was punished. He withdrew me from school, from 1939 to 1940. I thought I wouldn't go back to school because there was no one to help me, apart from that he was not in favour. One day he questioned me, why did you leave government school up there at the Station, to go down to mission school? I am the Fon, I build a school. You refuse the school. You go to a school built by an ordinary man or a quarter head. Is that proper? How can you go to mission school? Why leave government school run by government, to go to ordinary people's school? Government school is high, mission school low. I said it is the same thing they teach in all the schools. He said no!! You see the government there and you see the mission there, you think who has power more than the other?

The matter was worsened by the fact that my elder brother, Joseph Fru-Asah Ndomu, who had been given a wife by my father in 1937, refused the wife, and married a wife for himself who was Catholic and in church fashion. This was enough to ruin my brother and his family in the eyes of my father, who never wanted it and died saying so. My brother too was very strong hearted and would not even explain himself and would not even beg for pardon. So when I left Government School Bamenda Station for Catholic Mission School Mankon, my father was offended. For that reason I left school.

Apart from my brother and me offending our father by going Catholic, 1937 was a good year for the family. We had been selling foodstuff at Ntambag, near where the Central Police District is situated today. There was the first market in Ntambag. My father and his large family produced quite a lot of foodstuff, and on the market day, we would all number over 50, carrying small baskets of cocoyams and various other types of food the family was producing to that market. And as luck was smiling on the family, the British administrator had noticed this large group of children – boys and girls, naked children – coming to sell in such large pairs. So, in 1937 the administrator appealed to my father, in view of the large quantities of food he brought to the market, if my father could feed the prisoners. He gave an offer to my father and my father accepted, to supply food to the inmates of Her Majesty's prison in Bamenda. We signed a contract – my father signed and so did the officer in charge of the prison. All the food we grew, and what we did not grew that was needed by the contractor, we had to buy and supply. All of us the family were involved, and the money we had was re-invested in buying things that we could not produce. Even with that, our father did not give us any money for our education and other needs.

For education and all other needs, my father relied on the uncles of the children to help. Since I had no viable uncles to help me, I turned to helping myself. I had one priest, quarter head of the area, late Ntse Castro, married to a cousin of mine. In 1938, he invited me to stay with him and his wife, so I left my age group with whom I was staying at the grass house we built, to stay with them. There I lived, and every weekend, I had to go to the Fon's farm to fetch firewood to sell at Ntambag. We also caught fish, mud fish, with hooks to sell to civil servants, the elites, the rich people in town, and with the money thus earned, I was able to buy a few things to maintain myself in school. Sometimes we had to draw water for the settlers at Ntambag, to make a little cash to buy pencil and exercise books. And so we lived on like that.

That 1938 was also the year we had a very trying moment in my father's palace. The Catholics were not happy with the type of marriage my father had. It was customary for certain dignitaries to give the Fo a wife, and for the Fo to accept their offers. That year my father was married to three wives, all of whom were Catholics. Then the church came in, and instigated the parents to claim that my father had forced their hand in marriage. My father was charged of rape, forceful marriage and so on. It was a serious thing, a serious blow to the family, and I was dropped from school, the Catholic Mission School I had opted to attend when I withdrew from Government School Bamenda where my father had sent me initially. My father asked me to come home, to accompany him to the court every day. I left school. And every day, I followed him, carrying his chair to the court. Accompanying my father on official outings or for special meetings around the palace was something I was quite used to, as, from the age of five, I had been trained on how to serve my father.

I would carry the chair to court, and stay by my father, following the proceedings. The court was very far from the palace, and as the case became very serious, we were forced to stay nearer to the court in order to attend sessions in time. In truth, the girls my father was being accused of raping and forced marriage were not minors; they were mature women betrothed to my father. He married them rightfully and lawfully, in accordance with the customs of the land. So we tried, in the British way of self-defence, to tell the truth as informed by our customs. We went into the details of the matter and with the evidence at our disposal. But when the premier investigations were through and my father was charged, we realized my father was in danger. I was there by him, interpreting to him some of the things I heard the magistrate say. When we left the court to go home, my father would ask me to narrate to him what was said in court, and I would tell him as much as possible what I gathered from my little knowledge of English at the time.

We came to a point where one of my father's fathers-in-law who was not in support of the case, withdrew his daughter from us, saying he did not give us a wife. The daughter was taken to Mambu Bafut, and hidden, until the case was resolved. She eventually came back to the marriage, and with my father had children (one of whom is Benedict Ntaralah, who today is father of several children and himself a Catholic Christian and custodian of Mankon customs and traditions). Two young women remained, the mother of Clement Mankefo and then the girl we got from Mbuh in Baforchu. With the latter the matter was more serious. When she was called to give evidence, she made the case incriminating my father. The magistrate asked the woman, 'had you sex with this man?' She said, 'Yes'. 'Did you like it?' She said, 'No', she was forced. She said she had been guided to my father's house by a few of my mothers, the elders, who had ensured my father had sex with her. Asked to confirm the story, my father said, 'No, I have never seen this woman'. He said the woman was just brought to the palace recently. He said she had never entered his own bedroom. The woman insisted, 'You know me, you had sex with me'. And then the magistrate said, 'Can you describe the Fo's bedroom?' The woman said, 'Yes', his bed is this way, this is the type of thing you find there, you find that, find that, find that. Then the magistrate decided to send a police man to prove the woman's allegations and gave a search warrant that the compound be searched. He adjourned the court till the next day, and we left. The person sent to verify the allegations was expected to report back the next day.

So while going home, I told my father what the magistrate had said. 'He said what?!!!!' exclaimed my father. 'If what this woman has said is true, then every other thing I have said is a lie.' When he saw that the police man dispatched to ascertain had a bicycle, he commanded: 'You go now to the palace. You run, you run to the palace. Tell them to dislodge the palace of everything. This man must not confirm anything that woman has said...»

I left the court running. I ran, I am not a good runner, but I did wonders on that day. As I came ahead, I gave information and said they should dislodge the palace and send the things into the forest before the policeman comes. And like one man, they went up, and I went to the forest. I went down there, I was so tired. I went sweating, and lay in there. In less than an hour, the palace was dislodged, by Mafo Ndefru III, my mothers, my sisters and everyone else present. Throughout the trial, the whole family was gathering here at the palace every day. Nobody went to the farm. It was just like somebody had died. So I went and reported to my father that I got here before the man riding the bicycle and that everything was done as he had directed.

The next day the court reopened and the policeman reported on what he had seen and what he had not seen.

My father was freed.

When we came back he said, well, today, I see the value of education, you go back.

That was all my father said. He did not even give my fees. He couldn't give. His principle was for children to rely on uncles for schooling and other needs. The fact that I had no uncles to rely on took little away from the principle.

However, as we were carrying food up to the prison, I met my school father, Reverend Father Macdonald. He said, 'Big Head, why are you not coming to school again?' I said, 'No school fees, no uniform.' He said, 'Come, come back.' I went and he gave me underwear and his knickers and I started school. He paid my school fees for one year.

So I went back to school. Because of my family background, my mother's only uncle couldn't do anything. He had to leave Mankon in 1938 to go and work in the plantations in order to find money to marry a wife. Whenever he was discussing with my mother, they were both crying. This made it clear to me that I had to fend for myself. I became wholly involved with the food supply business, and worked daily with the clerk, the store man and all the others in the chain. This worked well for me, as it was done mostly early in the morning and after school.

The business prospered, and in 1938, we bought a lorry to convey some of the produce. We named the lorry 'Aghanwi' (God's Gift); we were the first people to own a lorry in the whole of the Bamenda region at the time. With the help of the lorry, we were going to Batibo to buy food, which had become big business for our family. We built a big warehouse around where my garage is today, and I was living there and taking care of business. At one point, the person in charge of feeding the prisoners resigned, and I had to combine his work with school and going to the prison yard with food. Sometimes I would leave very early in the morning to buy food items for breakfast and meals for the inmates. In this way I became acquainted with most households – buying garri, buying corn flour and things that we couldn't supply from the palace – and with butchers and dealers in other foodstuffs we needed to keep our business running.

Back in Government School Bamenda Station, I was elected school head boy. We had a farm and I was put as gardener and as treasurer, I kept the money. My keen interest in agriculture, coupled with my careful handling of money from the farm sales in the school, impressed the school authorities. In Standards 5 and 6, my Headmaster, Adekoke Adelabo, a Nigerian, was very impressed with me. After classes at Government School Bamenda Station, when I crossed over to the prison he followed me, he watched what I was doing. My Headmaster used to accompany me to the prison yard where I would go every afternoon after school till 6 o'clock. I was given four workers from the palace to carry food there, and I gave instructions for people to weigh the food and all.

Impressed, Mr Adekoke Adelabo advised me to apply to go to college when I successfully completed Standard Six in 1944, the top most class in Government School Bamenda Station. At that time, our only college was Saint Joseph's College, Sasse, Buea. I didn't even like to go to Sasse because I had been shown that a Catholic school was not a very good school. So, with the encouragement of my Headmaster, I registered for an entrance exam to a school in Nigeria – the Aggrey Memorial College, Arochuku, Eastern Nigeria. And the results came back and I passed. I was admitted. But there was no money to go to college. I told my father my good news, but he said there was no money. His philosophy about school and schooling had not changed. My Headmaster could not believe it when I told him. He said, 'What?!!!!' I said, 'There is no money.' I said, 'I told my father and he says there is no money.' He grew angry. He asked if I was paid for all the work I did for my father every day. I said, 'How can my father pay me?' He said, 'Your father didn't pay you and cannot pay your fees?' He said, 'I will see him... I want to see him, I want to see him.'

Then Mr Adekoke Adelabo took me down to the palace. My father was in when we came, and I introduced my Headmaster. He said, 'this pikin, this pikin he will go to big school in Nigeria, you say you don't have money?' He asked my father to produce the money. He told my father, 'every day I will find him in prison working and giving food to prisoners, and there carrying the things to prison, weighing them and every month you come and carry a lot of money. Where is that money? Why is it you have no money? I am going to report you to the D.O. for the years and money this young man has worked, you have to pay him.' He asked the Fo, if it was another man would you not pay?' The Fo said he would pay. The

Headmaster asked, 'how much were you paying the first man who was doing the job before he resigned?' My father told him, 4 pounds 10 shillings. 'And why wouldn't you pay this young man for the same work done?' he asked. 'We will check all that money and if you don't pay him, I am going to report you to the D.O., he insisted. The man was talking with spit coming out from his mouth. He talked very hard, the Yoruba man, and left, still angry.

When Mafo Ndefru III came from the farm, my father narrated the story. He, referring to the charges of rape and forced marriage, said, 'I have just finished with this case of women, and now this boy comes with his own case. Mafo, we are in trouble. If we don't let this boy go, I will be again in trouble.' They all resolved to allow me go.

I left for Nigeria, poor me. But, as I was later to realise, many others who would play a part in the region in future turned out to have gone to Nigeria for further education. Amongst these were John Ngu Foncha, Emmanuel M.L. Endeley, N.N. Mbile and Bernard Fonlon.

In 1946, Mafo Ndefru III went to Lagos. A friend talked to her about the charms and attractions of the city of Lagos, and she decided to go there and experience it for herself. As one of the prominent financial contributors to the Nigerian War Relief Fund in November 1944, she did not see why Lagos should be known to her only through the experiences of others. Here in Mankon, Mafo was a respected woman. She was the king of women, and she had never travelled. So there she was taking the train, being elbowed, having to carry her own luggage, and being pushed down, when she would ordinarily have my father's wives and the children carrying her bag and so on. In Lagos she was treated just like a slave. Nothing there – sleeping and eating in hotels, shabby treatment, having to fend for herself – remotely resembled the honour and respect she was used to back home. There when she was not staying and eating in hotels, she was trekking to and from the house they stayed, and going to fetch water for herself, when back here she would have all the attention she deserved. She was so upset, and the harshness of life in Lagos affected her mentally. My father learnt of it and sent two persons to bring her home, and she came back safely. When I came home for fees, I found her mad, being treated.

She eventually recovered. Mafo Ndefru III recovered very well. It was just this change of environment that gave her the shock. In fact she died ten years after I became Fo Mankon. Born in 1893, she had lived her life, and had excelled at her functions as administrator of the women and children of the palace, entertainer and feeder of palace visitors, counsellor of the Fo on certain matters of administration of the Kingdom, and spokeswoman for and liaison between Mankon women and the palace. The problem she had when I took over was that of cataract – the eyes. Fortunately, I brought a specialist, a medical doctor, who cured her, and I paid 50 pounds. Pleased with what he had done, I gave him a plot in the layout there. We were so happy that Mafo Ndefru III was able to see again. She was able to see me for the first time, since I became Fo Mankon. She guided me for 10 years, before passing away in 1970. She was laid to rest in her tomb near the palace. So, Mafo Ndefru III did survive her Lagos experience, but we had lost the job of feeding the prisoners.

Although my father had given me his blessings to enrol at the Aggrey Memorial College, he could not pay my fees because his contract with the government to supply food to prisoners was abruptly terminated. A very kind man, Mr. P.P Gray gave me one year scholarship, so I went back to Nigeria. One teacher, R. Teku, who taught us in the Government School Bamenda Station, happened to be a villager in the area where I schooled in Nigeria. He had retired. When he saw me, he was pleased, and made available to me a piece of land to farm. I welcomed the opportunity, and divided my time between school and the farm. I was very popular there, and was appointed the Janitor of the college experimental farm and library, which meant that I stayed in the dormitory. During holidays, I couldn't go home. There was no transport money again, and there was the Nigerian Railway strike. The small money sent to me from home was missing. I explained my situation to the Vice Principal, so the yams I grew all went back to the school when I harvested, and from this I earned a little money to keep going. Times were hard, but there was no giving up.

The hard work and determination paid off. I took four instead of the statutory five years to obtain the Cambridge School Certificate and a certificate in Agriculture. On graduation, I received a testimonial from the principal and proprietor of the college, Mr Alvan Ikoku, dated 31 December 1950 that read:

> This is to certify that Solomon Ndefru was a student here from 1946 to 1950. He passed secondary class five in 1949 and studied a further year (1950) in class six.
>
> He was elected College prefect in 1950 by both staff and students and has revealed great qualities of leadership and responsibility in bearing what is regarded as the highest honour of the school.
>
> Solomon is loyal without losing his right of criticism, sensible and honest. His courtesy and sense of humour make him a great winner through. I expect great things of him in the wider life beyond the College campus.

When I completed college and returned home, I took the civil service examination in my quest for employment. My father said he would like me to be D.O. or to go work with the D.O. My aunt said she would want me to work in the hospital. I did not reveal that I had written the civil service examination, and that my option was agriculture. There was my wife's cousin, who was working as an overseer, with the Government Agricultural Experimental Farm in Bambui. Through him we learnt of the possibilities of employment. He told us they were recruiting workers for fieldwork, but they wanted a level of qualification much lower than what I had obtained. The highest education we had then was the Level 3 – the certificate for those who had gone into Saint Joseph's College Sasse for three years – Senior Cambridge. And we learnt that anybody who had got Senior Cambridge would only be employed as director.

Then we decided that I will tell the people recruiting that I had written the examination for the Junior Cambridge and that I was waiting for the results. We decided that was what I was going to say. Fortunately for me, the agricultural superintendent in charge of the farm was married to the sister of one of my teachers at college. This girl had known me, whilst I was in college. So when she saw me, she said, 'what, who is this?' I said, 'this is my home.' She took me to refer to the husband, who asked me about his home, the college and people I knew. I described what I did, the country, and talked to him about people we both knew very well. The man offered me a temporary job as record keeper. As record keeper, I was travelling to all the farms in and around Buea – from lower farms to upper farms. I was in the office keeping records, and out in the farms seeing the plots, and seeing the people in there. I was enjoying the work. I can't remember now what I was earning.

One day while I was at upper farms, I heard someone was looking for me. The results of the examinations I took when I left school had been published. The Commissioner of the Public Service, employing civil servants in Lagos, had sent a telegram that I should report to the Higher School of Agricultural Techniques (Moor Plantation) in Ibadan, Nigeria, with immediate effect. Incidentally, this was the same school where John Ngu Foncha studied between 1941 – 1943. I went to the office before heading home. There, my colleague said, 'ha massa na so you dey? Why you no been tell we say na so you know book?' They wanted to know how I managed to write Senior Cambridge, and why I had kept the matter a secret. I told them I didn't know I was going to pass the exam, so there was no point sharing the fact of writing it. Those who had been treating me like a small clerk for reporting were now full of respect towards me. Automatically, I was above them by rank, by my qualification.

When I had my certificate, following an agreement I had with Mr. Njuh, we wrote an application in April, and by August I was employed and immediately I left by 20 August 1951. I was overseer in 1950. I was already employed from Enugu as overseer by the director – around 1April. Then by August, the final employment results from Enugu came – That was the rank for Junior Cambridge people. I was now to go to Ibadan School of Agriculture. Thus, in August 1951, I returned to Nigeria for a two year course in Ibadan. I had learnt my lesson, I wanted to work and pay myself. As far as I could remember, that had always been so. When I attended primary school under the missionaries, I used to keep a tomato garden and to grow cabbages as well. While I was in school, I was doing so many little jobs to earn some small money for my primary education, and my father really helped me when I was working for him, even when he was not paying me for the work I did. In that way, I was able to buy my books and pay for everything for school.

I graduated in 1953 and was awarded a diploma as an Agricultural Assistant Grade III. I returned home in 1954.

Going to school meant that I was hardly around the palace. For that reason, I never thought I could be Fo Mankon. Many of my brothers were hanging around. I was hardly here. They were always here. So I thought those who were there would be Fo Mankon someday.

2

The Big Surprise

I came back from training and reported back at the farm. I was to be Farm Manager. Then I heard that I was going to open a new station; that they were to propose to send me to Mambila or somewhere. It came that I should go and work at the station in the then Menchum Division, which today has been split into Menchum and Boyo Divisions. I went there, and I had a lot to do. I opened an experimental farm in Befang. There I nursed oil palm seeds and coffee and distributed them to local farmers to plant. I also experimented with cocoa, by nursing the seedlings and distributing them to local farmers of the Menchum Valley. My area of jurisdiction extended to the Kom area. Feeder experimental farms were established at Naikom, Esimbi, Weh, Esu, and Wum, and in Abu, Njinikom, Bello and Meli in Kom.

I wanted to impress. I was sure one day one of my directors would come to see what I was doing. By initiative I started things that were good, but that I wasn't asked to do. Once I had made my initial observations I asked for some money to do this and so on. I opened individual demonstration plots for the chiefs of the places and members of parliament working there, asking them to use these as model farms to encourage their populations to embrace modern farming techniques. I worked closely with the people of the area, and established demonstration farm plots for some individual farmers who were grateful. Amongst them were late Lucas Akwa Neng of Weh, Hon. J.C. Kum of Befang, Mewele Boja of Modelle and late Bangho of Esu. However, given the large area I had to cover, coupled with the poor road infrastructure of the 1950s, I had difficulties moving from one demonstration farm plot to the other. Very often, I travelled around by bicycle, motorcycle, and on foot.

My director in Buea, Mr D.G.M. Hutchison – Southern Cameroon Director of Agriculture, to whom I reported regularly, came on field inspection visits and saw all those things, and was impressed. In August 1956 I was promoted to Agricultural Assistant Grade II, followed in September 1958 by another promotion to Agricultural Assistant Grade I. Salary-wise these promotions did not mean much, given the relatively low pay in the civil service, but the job satisfaction was great, and the feeling of recognition and achievement total. This brought me happiness, and spurred me to work even harder. I enjoyed certain rights and privileges, such as touring allowances and free medical care.

I came and build a house here at SONAC Street, just as I built my house there in Menchum Division, where I loved the work I was doing. I thought I would retire much earlier to do my own work at home. I acquired part of the plot where Ngen-mbo village is currently located when my father was still alive, and planted some palms there, long before part of the land was given to them in 1954.

The big surprise was when I came here to submit my report at the head office. When I arrived, I called to greet my father as usual. He was having a fever. We started a conversation, but I couldn't understand him. I was wearing a pair of shoes, and we started talking about shoes. He said, 'you have big feet like my own. This your own shoes, can you not give me this?' 'If you can wear them,' I said. Then he said, 'give me this.' I told him my wife had prepared some provisions for the palace. I had brought some rice, some dried fish, and so on. He said, 'go and thank your woman.' I said, 'before I go back, I want to go and see the doctors whether they can give something for you to take for this your fever. I went and consulted and was prescribed medicine for him, which I brought back. Then he started recovering.

I went away.

Just two weeks after I left my father, David, my third child, was born. I came back to ask my father for a name for my son. I informed him my wife has put to birth, a baby boy. He said, 'Oh! That's me, name him after me.' I said, 'Ok.' Then he asked, 'How long will you be here? I told him. He asked, 'Have you built your house?' I said, 'Yes, I have a house there.' He said, 'where?' I said I had a house in SONAC Street. I said, 'If I come and live there, you can come and we chat there.' Then he told me, it was advisable to get somebody to help me now that my wife had given birth to a baby boy. I told him that I had four babysitters in the house. As I travelled a lot, I had four men who worked with me, and who travelled with me. As I work from Division to Division, from village to village, I have servants in my house, I had cooks in my house, and I had lots of people coming and going.

My father said that was not the sort of help he meant. He meant a woman. He said he wanted me to take a second woman. Oh! Then I told him, 'Mbeh, I don't think I will marry two wives. The work is too difficult for me to have two wives.' He said, 'Hmm, you will marry only one wife?' Not waiting for me to answer he added, 'If all of you marry only one wife, all these ones I have here, where will they go if I am no more?' I said, 'Well, as I have been constant to supply you all help for you, helping your wives and children, whoever is here, I will do same. But for me, I don't think I need a second wife.'

Then I left. It was mid March 1959.

Two weeks after, I receive word that my father had summoned all of us to appear here at the palace urgently, that he had rallied us home. The message I got was simple: 'Better no dey, better no dey,' meaning, as far as I could gather, that his illness had grown worse.

Hardly did I suspect my father had died.

I rushed home. In less than no time I was there, tired but happy to have responded to the call as fast as I could. They said we should retire to my mother's house. I had only my hand bag. I thought I was only coming to help the way I was used to – going for consultations, getting prescriptions and buying my father's drugs. I was thinking of paying bills, of a motor car, of rushing him to hospital. I was thinking of everything but the fact that my father had died.

Sensing from the crowds and tension in the air that my father's situation had grown severe, I asked them to allow me to see him so I could rush back to my office and ask for permission to stay longer and take care of him until he had fully recovered his health. No one I talked to gave my words any attention. They merely asked me to stay put. It seemed as if the whole of Mankon had migrated to live here at the palace. We were having a common meal and now staying here. For those who lacked bedding, they will go and sleep at their homes and early in the morning they will come to continue with the business of being concerned. There I was with them, in the dark, without access to my father, and not quite knowing how critically his health had deteriorated. My father had never given or discussed a will with me. I had never been told at any time I will be here as Fo Mankon one day. So I was not in anyway, expecting anything that happened. I thought it would be the formality, that I would come, attend to his urgent medical needs, have his health re-established, and go back to my station. That was not to be.

Although confined in the palace since my arrival from Befang, I was finally told that my father would see me, and I was guided from my mother's house to the palace by elderly notables. Still, I suspected nothing, as I thought the extra security around my movements had simply been imposed by the fact of my father's deteriorating health.

It all dawned on me however, when I was arrested and carried away the moment I climbed the steps into the inner palace. It was the greatest surprise in my life.

All my personal programmes destroyed. I had planned to go to Ibadan to continue my studies in Agriculture by April, only for my father to pass away on 31 March. When I was taken and confined, my department and director were immediately notified. General Tataw, who was the pay clerk at the time, came here at the end of the month with my salary. Mr D.G.M. Hutchison, the director of agriculture, told me I could either resign or come back to resume work after my installation. Personally, however, I was not happy with the turn things were taking in my life. Although my mother had, in my upbringing, taken time to school me in the ways and values of the land, and had made sure that the traditions, customs and etiquette of the palace were well internalized by me, I didn't want to be Fo Mankon.

I was also ignorant of what the whole thing was about. I believed my brothers were more qualified and was ready to concede the title to any of my junior brothers who was interested. I was promising to pay half of my salary or part salary to help whoever brother would take the throne. Had any of my brothers shown interest, I would certainly have done all to pass onto him the challenge of stepping into our father's shoes. There were no contenders, even if, as was to surface much later, Brain Sharwood-Smith, the Senior Divisional Officer for Bamenda Division at the time, upon being informed by the king makers that '*nmogh nwuegh bienneugh* (The Fon is Missing)' had sought to influence events by writing to inform and instruct my elder brother Joseph Fru-Asah Ndomu thus:

... your father, the Fon, is late since March 30, 1959. The enthronement is due soon. You are, therefore, requested to make all arrangements to be at home before the 1st of April. ..... My interest is that from your acceptable administrative qualities you should be the heir to the throne. I will also do everything at my level to influence your acceptance by the Mankon traditional king-makers although they may have an alternative...

It was an instruction my brother clearly ignored, as he was present at the enthronement not to contest but to honour the will of our father. I knew nothing about the SDO's letter and preference, having been caught and confined in the palace as soon as I came from Befang in response to the urgent summons on the critical situation of my father. So for quite a long time, I was undecided. Mankon has only one Fo, there cannot be two. The Fo assisted by the kwi'fo, Nda Bukum and Takumbeng manage the affairs of the community. Unlike other Kingdoms in the Grassfields, there are no second class Fons in Mankon. Eight king makers were there to convince and to guide me. All the big men, I was sleeping with them in the same house. The king makers were living together, to monitor my movements. Determined to fulfil my father's will, they didn't want the chosen one to spring a surprise on them. I was confined.

As I continued to resist, one day Mafo Ndefru III came, stood behind me, outside there and asked me to come forth. I went along, near where I have planted the plum tree behind the inner palace. She told me that, she learnt I am not happy. She learnt I am not looking well, and I refuse to eat. 'The report is not a good report,' she said. But to avert herself any rumours or blame, she continued, 'I have done just what your father told me to do.' She said, 'If there is anybody saying another thing, my hands are clean – it is your father's will. It's not any of us interested, it is not by election. So if you are unhappy, if you don't take your meals, it's not my fault. Know that I have implemented your father's will.' Then she left.

The following day, the senior women also obtained permission to see me. Nobody was seeing me that time, they had to come inside. My mother was amongst them. They said, 'Well, we have heard that you don't want to stay, that you want to go back to your work. What will become of Mankon if you do that?' They were two women appointed to attend to me, to take care of my emotions. I tried to talk them into seeing with me. 'You know I was always saying that I will like to go back to school,' I told them. But they reiterated their position. 'We have now heard all the reports of what is happening. We are your mothers telling you. Your father has left us in your hands. We hear you like your work so much you want to go back to your work, and from there help us. We want to tell you that, by going back to your work, your father left us with nobody. And when you go, we too will follow him. Whatever you send you send to whom? We will not be here to eat anything you send. But take note that what has been done by the tradition on you, if you leave this place now, you will never step foot on Mankon land again. You can never be an ordinary man. You will be dining with nobody, you will have discussions with nobody, no njangi house will admit you – nothing. So whatever you have, how can it ever come to us? You can never associate with the Mankon society in anyway. So don't talk only of your father's troubles. We are now, we your mothers, we are left only to follow him.'

I was touched. I went back in, touched.

So I told myself, 'let me take up courage and see whether I can do this thing. At thirty-four years of age, I was confirmed Fo Mankon.

The day was April 4, and the enthronement started around midday. The palace was bustling with people from Mankon and well-wishers from places near and distant. The entrance into the palace was lined on both sides by the population, men mostly in front, women and children behind. I was led out of the palace by eight king makers and two *menang* masquerades (wearing woven grass and a robe), and walked gradually and silently through the passage lined thick with people. In tune with tradition, I was wearing only the *ntum* – a white cloth around my waist passed between my legs and connected with a white band as a belt around my waist. In my hand I carried a staff made of bamboo, with two red feathers stocked on the upper end, to symbolize both the killing of a leopard or buffalo and the unity of the Kingdom of Mankon. I followed closely behind the two *menang*, tall with dignity bolstered by my height and solid build. The king makers, wearing *mindore* – climbing plants – round their necks, followed me. I was the only person not dressed in mourning attire.

As we approached the population of mourners, *menang* stepped aside, clearing the way for me and the eight king makers to go into the crowd. We moved around the plaza, making it possible for me to acknowledge and salute the people, and for the people see me at close range and even to touch me. I was just getting used to it when the *menang* caught up with me and touched me. I got the cue and started retreating to the palace. Why walk back became a run, to symbolize seeking refuge from stoning. Shouting and screaming, the people ran forward joyously trying to pelt me with little stones and clod of dirt. This was mean to instil confidence and fortify me for the challenges of leadership that I will have to face as Fo Mankon. Gun firing, suspended during the period of mourning, resumed as the people awaited my naming as a Fo.

In the interval, the population of mourners and well-wishers briefly retired home or went to nearby streams to bath and prepare themselves for the naming ceremony. When we reappeared at the plaza early in the afternoon, I was dressed in royal regalia. The population had assembled with their guns, spears and cutlasses. I sat on a large elevated rostrum in the plaza. As was customary, I was named after one of my predecessors – Angwafo, and since two had already borne the title before me, I became Fo Angwafo III of Mankon. This made of me the 20th Fo Mankon. The first Angwafo was the 18th Fo Mankon. He was succeeded by Fomukong, who in turn handed over to Angwafo II, the father of Tata Laboerü, who became Ndefru III in 1919. A complete list of Fo, together with the story of origin and migration of Mankon people, is available in the background publication we prepared in 1984 (see pp.20-24), towards the Nükwi Nü Fo Ndefru III, a commemorative cultural festival in honour of my late father.

When the king makers proclaimed the name of the twentieth Fo Mankon, the population erupted. There was ululation, singing, drumming and dancing by groups from clans and quarters all over Mankon. People came forward and saluted me ceremoniously by displaying their gun butts, spears and cutlasses in the air. I got up and danced with the population, going round from one group to another. Then, prompted by the king makers, I retired to the inner palace in their company.

Following this formal enthronement and naming, I was then introduced to the population. All the traditional group members were behind me, bringing their presents to me, introducing their various families. I was being introduced to all the societies in Mankon. Through with the introductions to the people of Mankon and to the wider population, I had to be introduced to the Administration, to say I can now work. I can now receive people and so on. So I was taken to where I was later to build the main market to meet the population.

Made to see that there was no turning back on my new role and direction in life, I formally relinquished my appointment in the Department of Agriculture. When Mr D.G.M. Hutchison, acting Director of Agriculture, Southern Cameroons, received by letter of resignation, he wrote back. His letter, dated 6 January 1960, read:

> Following your succession to the stool of your late father, it was necessary for you to relinquish your appointment in the Department of Agriculture in order to take up your duties as Fo Mankon.
>
> I wish to convey to you my great appreciation of the long and faithful service which you have given to the Department.
>
> After joining the Department as a Field Overseer in April, 1951, you rapidly made progress and in August 1951 were appointed Agricultural Assistant; by diligent and painstaking application to your work you were able to assist materially in the development of improved agricultural practices, particularly in the Wum area; your work gained you well-merited promotion to the rank of Agricultural Assistant Grade I, and this was the rank you held on retirement.
>
> Whilst I regret the necessity of your having to leave the Department in mid-career, I am confident that by your example you will continue to further the cause of modern agriculture in your area and I trust that your people will continue to benefit from your knowledge and advice for many years to come.

That was where the whole journey started. I began my career as a ruler, and as a politician.

3

The Plebiscite: My Initiation into Politics

Normally, my confinement should have been for about six months, during which period I was to learn or reappraise myself with palace protocol and etiquette, and be introduced and initiated into the cultural and political institutions and regulatory societies of Mankon by the king makers.

Circumstances however forced me to make a premature outing from the palace. The plebiscite matter had come up and the commissioner had appointed me to play a central role. He said, 'the Fon of Mankon, you are one of the traditional rulers appointed to determine the question of the plebiscite. The first meeting was to be in Mamfe. So we had to organize. I toured all the divisions to have them express their opinions as to the questions of the plebiscite. I had to attend the preparatory conference held in Mamfe from 10-11 August 1959, scheduled to lay the foundation for the February 11 1961 Plebiscite in the Southern Cameroons. Just before leaving for Mamfe, I was introduced to the wider population – both Mankon and settler – at Ntambag. I was taken to meet with a cross-section of the settler population of Mankon urban area at the Community Hall, on July 30 1959. The occasion, which took the whole day at the end of which I was led back to the palace, stands out in my mind for the huge crowds that stood on both sides of the Commercial Avenue to salute me as I drove in. The Community Hall was full to capacity. I was touched by the reception I got from the Mankon population and settler community alike.

When my father passed away on March 31 1959, I was the returning officer for an election in Ndung area in Kom, along with Ngom Jua and others. We went to Achain and several other villages in the area. So, if I had anything to do with elections, it was then that it started. I was more or less initiated into politics in the elections of March. By November 1959, it was the question of the plebiscite, and I was appointed to tour all the Divisions in this region, explaining to them what they needed to know to be able to make informed decisions. At the August 10-12 Mamfe conference chaired by Sir Sidney, and held to discuss the questions of the plebiscite, the choice was limited to two questions: *Do you wish to achieve independence by joining the independent Federation of Nigeria? Or, Do you wish to achieve independence by joining* the independent Republic of Cameroun.' I took the floor and spoke in favour of reunification with the Republic of Cameroon, the territory formerly administered by the French.

The elections for the Southern Cameroon House of Chiefs followed in 1960. I stood for the elections to represent the Ngemba people in the House of Chiefs, which I won by twelve out of fifteen votes, defeating one other candidate. The Fon of Bafut and the Fon of Bali however did not contest the elections; they went into the Southern Cameroon House of Chiefs as ex-officio members, given their recognition by the government of the day at the time as 'First Class Fons'. In early 1961, prior to the plebiscite, the first Southern Cameroon Chiefs Conference was held, during which the chiefs pledged their support for John Ngu Foncha's KNDP, the ruling party. In the conference, elections were conducted during which the Fon of Bafut, the Fon of Bali and myself were elected president, vice president and treasurer respectively.

I was more or less a leader in the House of Chiefs, followed by the Fon of Bafut. Even though there were older people, few of them had studied or even tried to get a paper or anything in the field of education. In addition to the studies I had done in school and college, I benefitted much from anthropologists, historians and others scholars and researchers who came by to study various aspects of Mankon traditions, customs and society. Discussions and conversations with them were most enriching. Some gave me a few books and so on. In those days I was still a young man and I was still interested in reading. My education and exposure to ideas brought a lot of hatred for me.

As a member of the House of Chiefs, I participated in campaigning for the Plebiscite of February1961, in which I was in favour of reunification with the Republic of Cameroon. Following the plebiscite were the elections into the West Cameroon House of Assembly. This was seen by some political parties as a new mandate to flush out those who didn't want reunification, from becoming members of parliament. These elections were going to take place on the 31st December 1961.

I was of the opinion that the Mankon voters, or voters of the lower Ngemba – that's Mankon, Chomba, Mbatu, Nsongwa – needed to choose a candidate. The leadership for all Ngemba people was my father. A little context is in order here. Following the terms of the 1919 treaty of the League of Nations after World War I, the Southern Cameroons, of which Mankon was a part, was administered as part of Eastern Nigeria. There was a Resident administrator stationed in Buea, assisted by a junior Resident administrator in Bamenda, and several District Officers in the respective Divisions. From 1922, the system of Indirect Rule was introduced throughout the Southern Cameroons. This was a system by which Britain administered the Southern Cameroons by using the Fons (chiefs) as agents and by utilizing existing traditional political institutions where these were found to be appropriate. The system involved the establishment of Native Administration Courts which tried civil cases while the Magistrate Courts tried criminal cases.

In 1927 the Ngemba Native Court was established and my father Fo Ndefru III and Mama of Baforchu were appointed presidents. Not pleased to be placed a step lower than the Fons of Bali, Kom, Bafut and Banso who were appointed District Heads of Native Authorities under the Indirect Rule system, my father, as leader of the most senior Kingdom in the Ngemba area wrote to the Commissioner at Enugu, requesting reclassification. Court III which later became the Mankon Village Group Court, took up the name of Mankon Customary Court and occupied the premises of the former Ngemba Native Court at Ntatruru. The President of this court was my father, who later transferred the court to its present site at Ntambag. In 1945 some members of the other courts complained bitterly about corruption and inefficiency. They made an appeal to the administration and Fo Ndefru III, to include them in the Mankon Customary Court. Their plan was accepted that same year and they were allowed to join the Mankon Court. These kingdoms were Baforchu II from Court I, Chomba, Mbatu and Nsongwa from Court II and Mundum I and II from Court VI. Today these kingdoms still share the same court with Mankon. While Mankon proper is today divided into 4 court wards, the other kingdoms together form the fifth court ward. The transformation by the British in 1949 of the Native Authority system into the local government system resulted in the establishment of local government for Mankon known as the Mankon Subordinate Native Authority or the Mankon Urban Council. This allowed for recognition and representation for various villages and interest groups, including women and strangers in the township. It was clearly stated in Article 8 of the Standing Rules of the Council that '... the Fon of Mankon shall be the one ex-officio President of the Council, and shall be President by virtue of his position as the Fon of Mankon.' This was an important development, as it brought back to the Fon some of the authority he had lost over Ntambag, the township area mostly occupied by administration, businesses and strangers.

When I took over from my father in 1959 and took up that office of President of the Ngemba Native Court, the political party leaders – the KNDP in particular –were so frightened. I was well educated both in the modern sense of schooling, and also in the ways and interests of the land of Mankon people and the neighbouring Kingdoms with whom we had enjoyed a long history of confederation and a common sense of strategic interests. Every time we met, these political party leaders monitored my position, aware as they were, of my popularity amongst the population of Ngemba. So when I made it known that I was going to run for parliament, that I wanted to represent my people in my chieftaincy capacity – consultant capacity – as a member of House of Chiefs that brought me a lot of trouble. John Ngu Foncha, who until then had associated me with his KNDP, made it clear he would not allow me to contest the elections as a member of the KNDP party for the Lower Ngemba constituency. Foncha preferred Daniel Awa Nangah who was a cousin to his wife, Anna Atang. As a businessman, Nangah was awarded most government contracts by Foncha. They wanted to keep political representation within their family circles. I wanted to save my people from dangerous rumours and victimization.

When I consulted with my people, they encouraged me to run as an independent. No Mankon politician had ever won an election before, even though there were Mankon leaders of political parties – Nde Ntumazah of One Kamerun (OK) party for example. Instead, Nde Ntumazah and his One Kamerun were perceived as a surrogate of the banned UPC, and therefore treated as a danger both by the authorities of the Republic of Cameroon and by the KNDP with whom it was competing for votes. Mankon had been accused of sympathizing with rebels, and the finger of suspicion and victimization pointed directly at Nde Ntumazah and his OK party, seen everywhere as the Anglophone version of the UPC which was engaged in a guerrilla war to overthrow the Ahidjo government. Nde Ntumazah and his activities were making people conclude that Mankon was pro-UPC and by implication anti-Ahidjo. I hated to see Mankon ignored the way Foncha's KNDP did, or made to pay for offering refuge to the violent ideas of a banned party when we had just voted to reunite the two Cameroons. I had to step in to ensure that Mankon was represented, and in a legitimate way.

The House of Assembly clearly had its advantages. When you get to the House, you can have a loan to buy a car. You are on a monthly stipend, you have the privilege allowance of having fuel in order to tour your constituency. Against what prevails in the House of Chiefs, you have a sitting fee. You may be consulted in the House of Chiefs, but your opinions don't have the same weight as the opinions of a member of parliament, who can actually influence government decisions and policies. So, although the KNDP did everything to suppress my election, I was not deterred. I went ahead with my campaign for parliament. The traditional iron twin gong was my campaign symbol as the independent candidate. It signified my call to the populations of Mankon and the entire Ngemba area to come out and support the person who best represented their interests and aspirations. I was gratified by the solidarity and unity of the population behind my campaign, solidarity and unity well captured in the campaign songs that they composed and reproduced wherever they went. The election took place, and when the votes were counted, I was declared the winner for the Lower Ngemba constituency. I had scored 3.376 votes, defeating another independent candidate – A.K. Ndikum, and three other candidates fielded by the KNDP (1.967 votes), OK (1,825 votes) and CPNC (235 votes). The Ok candidate was another Mankon citizen, the late Maximus Chibukom. When parliament opened in 1962, I was sworn in, but that didn't come easy.

I was approached to resign my position in parliament or as a Fon, by people who felt that I could not be both. These were people whose parties had contested the election against me as an independent, and whom I had beaten. When my supporters advised me to reconcile with the KNDP following the elections, I was willing to consider the suggestion, but John Ngu Foncha turned it down saying the loyalty of the people of Mankon was questionable. I insisted on keeping to the mandate given to me by my people to be an independent Member of Parliament and to protect their interests. Even then, they did everything to make sure that I shouldn't take the oath of office. John Ngu Foncha as chairman of the KNDP party whose candidate I had defeated at the elections, said a lot of political derogatory things about me and tried to make my people unhappy: 'The Fon is now a beggar, he is no longer a Fon'; 'The Fon has been stripped of his position and is now a mere floor member.' He did quite a lot to forestall my swearing in. But I heavily insisted that I couldn't help Foncha the way he wanted because as a single member constituency, my votes were very clear. I was so popular, beating four other candidates who stood against me.

On the opening day of parliament, the party consulted to form a government – J. N. Foncha's KNDP and Dr E.M.L Endeley's KNC. I was also consulted as an independent, and with my support, J.N. Foncha was appointed Prime Minister.

Even then, Foncha and the KNDP were still not happy with me. They thought they could get the majority of strangers in Mankon to vote against me at the election. It didn't work for the simple reason that strangers owed a lot to the open door policy of encouraging strangers to settle in Mankon, initiated since the reign of Fon Angwafo II, my grandfather. For example, Fon Angwafo II settled Mbanga of Bum and his followers at the southern end of Ntambag and provided them with enough farmland. He also accepted and built 29 houses at the northern end of Ntambag to accommodate a displaced group of Hausas under their leader Mallam Mama, when a fort was built at Müshüg. It was this open door policy and the influx of Hausas from Nigeria that attracted people from various origins, who engaged themselves mainly in commerce, construction and manufacturing.

Francophone Cameroonians, mostly Bamileke, who came seeking refuge or opportunity, were easily accommodated by my father, especially following the partition of Cameroon after World War I. Even when an attempt was made to repatriate the Francophones who had sought refuge in his Kingdom, Ndefru III objected, arguing that he was entitled as a Fon, to offer protection to these people. The fact that the rest of Mankon was still largely inhabited by Mankon people earning their living mostly from farming, hunting and fishing by no means meant that Fo Mankon should be indifferent to strangers.

Even the fact that some of those we welcomed developed leadership ambitions of their own, sometimes even going as far as challenging Mankon authority over Mankon township, was not reason enough for us to reverse the principle and open door policy of making strangers feel welcome in Mankon. So Ntambag became the eye and ear of Mankon in the modern urban world, meant to link the rural and the urban in continuous dialogue and interdependence. When it came to taxes, the British administration soon realized the importance of Mankon, and although there were occasional tensions when colonial administrator tried to behave as if the Mankon township belonged more to the British Crown than to Fo Mankon. So how could settlers or strangers, welcomed with open arms since the days of my grandfather, Angwafo II, turn around to vote against Angwafo III, whose only ambition was to consolidate their gains through seeking recognition and representation for Mankon as their landlord?

Having thus failed to beat me at elections, in 1962, they proposed a new law to reshape inter-village boundaries that was clearly targeted at Mankon. They claimed that Mankon was occupying the lands of neighbouring Kingdoms such as Bali, Bafut and Nkwen land. They decided to have Mankon divided into two. Fortunately for Mankon, the law died when multiparty politics gave way to the single party in 1966. I was accused of being arrogant, of having no respect for the Prime Minister, since I saw the Prime Minister to be no royalty like myself, as being just an ordinary citizen from Nkwen.

In January 1963, all the chiefs in Southern Cameroon were convened by the West Cameroon Chiefs Conference. Only I was literate, together with the Fon of Bafut, who was nominally educated. The suggestion was made that a commoner become Secretary to the Chiefs Conference. I raised an objection and said, 'How can that be? If this Chiefs Conference means anything, is there no chief who can be secretary?' So we met in Kumba, after all the failures at the campaign to dissuade me from contesting elections. And after the many manoeuvres with the Head of State to see whether they could flaw my swearing in. At the meeting in Kumba, they decided they wanted to try me. I was guilty for disobeying them and for proceeding to contest the election. The chiefs of the South West, voted in favour of my winning the elections and rather preferred that I pay some drinks and meat, may be one or two cows as penalty for having gone against the decision and wishes of the chiefs by contesting and winning elections. The Fon of Bali, who had a majority of the chiefs, voted in favour of my expulsion from the Chiefs Conference.

However, Foncha and the KNDP were overtaken by events. KNDP split into two. Solomon Tandeng Muna formed the CUC, and Foncha was losing grip of the people. And when Ahidjo saw this mushrooming of parties in West Cameroon, he formed the Cameroon National Union (CNU). Thus, I remained an independent member of the West Cameroon House of Assembly from 1962 to 1966, when multiparty politics were abolished following the institution of the one party system. I joined the CNU. In 1967, on the ticket of the Cameroon National Union, the single party, I was re-elected for parliament. Foncha said that I will not take my seat even if I won, because, according to him, the chief cannot be a member of parliament. But now he didn't have only me to deal with. Other Fons were speaking out. The Fon of Bafut said if he had contested elections in Bafut, they would vote for him, not for a man from Nkwen.

The House of Chiefs continued and there was still sitting fees, but the chiefs again were not happy because this time, as a Member of Parliament, I had my new car. That created a lot of tension, bitterness, this time against Mr Foncha who had supported the campaign against me and told them that even if I won the election they would unseat me, they wouldn't allow me. He had failed during the first multiparty election after independence, and now again, following the institution of the single party, he failed to stop me from taking up my seat. While my fellow chiefs continued on a sitting fees basis in the House of Chiefs in 1967, I was on a monthly salary. I had the privileges of a parliamentarian. I was given my car. I was paid my full salary. My prerogatives as a Member of Parliament the members of the House of Chiefs hadn't. That was the next problem. They turned to Foncha and said, 'You deceived us when you said even if this man wins elections you have the way to unseat him.' Fortunately for me, elections were not by the list system; I contested for a single member constituency, so Foncha could not use the list system to eliminate me.

That did not stop Foncha from accusing me and instigating others to accuse me of breaking the chiefs' law by going to parliament or doing politics. Before the end of that mandate, we were now to establish a single parliament. For economic reasons, we said instead of a West Cameroon House of Assembly, an East Cameroon House of Assembly, and the Cameroon National Assembly, we should have only the Cameroon National Assembly.

That took place in 1972. The House of Chiefs was abolished. The two houses of assembly too were abolished. And then in 1973, the national assembly was opened, and I had won the elections – and that was it – the greatest hatred I had ever known. Foncha's supporters and all the chiefs forced the Head of State to make the 1977 law, to classify chiefs, in order to make sure that they have their allowances and keep out of running for office in electoral politics. Prior to its abolition, there were only 37 Fons in the House of Chiefs, so many of them 'Second Class', few 'First Class'. I had the mandate and money for sometime – again they cried that I am having double salary. The problem was that I was taking my parliamentary salary and also my chieftaincy allowance. So by 1982 a law came out that I should choose one or the other – I cannot be paid two salaries on the same voucher more or less. So I gave up my chieftaincy allowance and I continued with that of Member of Parliament until 1988 when I retired from parliament.

The institution of the single party and re-unification in 1972 brought Solomon Tandeng Muna to centre stage in regional and national politics. Muna was an elderly man to me – he was teaching while I was still in school. The idea of modern politics started about 1950. The first elections to parliament were conducted in 1951, then you had the Bamenda and South West Federation – Native Authority, and my father was head of that federation. He supported Muna in the elections and Muna won. He also helped Muna resolve their land problem, in the same way that he had spearheaded their case for land which the Bali people had seized. At the time I came into politics, Muna was still a member of the KNDP. I surprised them, when I contested election as an independent. He was one of those who sought to dissuade me, but when I stood and won, Muna wasn't vocal. So that helped him maintain with me the same cordial relations he had with my father. He was very appreciative of what my father had done for them – going to war to make land available for their settlement – Ngen-mbo Village.

When the Federal Parliaments were abolished and the National Assembly created, I stood for elections and won. That meant going to Yaounde when we were in session, and where Muna was speaker. Luckily for me at the time, he had a prominent place and good accommodation. So he had spare accommodation for visitors, which he left to me. It solved all my problems – lodging me always whenever I went there. So instead of going to the hotel, moving from here and there, I had a permanent accommodation in his quarters.

Muna was a very meticulous man. He kept the badges for every meeting or conference he ever attended at home or abroad. He was also very grateful to Mankon, for the assistance my father gave his people, and for the solidarity and good will that have always characterised relations between Ngen-mbo and Mankon.

4

Fo Mankon and Politician

Some people say being a Fon and participating in politics are incompatible roles. They are entitled to their opinion, but I see things differently. I have a different understanding of my role as Fo Mankon and my role as a politician. I think a politician is one who rules people and Fo Mankon is the one who guides and keeps the traditions and customs of the Mankon people as a ruler. So, as far as politics is concerned, whether I am a politician or not, the sphere of activities include politics – all in one.

As I have already indicated, my becoming Fon coincided with the campaign for the plebiscite. I was drafted into the process. I was appointed to the commission that tried to draw up questions for that plebiscite and then decided to support those for re-unification. I was already doing politics as Fon. And after the plebiscite in February 1961, I went to parliament as an independent, beating all the other candidates that stood on the ticket of the various political parties. That was where my troubles started. Calls for my resignation came from the parties that felt I had cheated them out of a parliamentary seat. I ignored the calls to resign either as an MP or as a chief by those who thought it was improper for a chief to hold an elected office. I refused to subscribe to the dichotomy between Fon and politician.

Upon the re-unification of the English and French Cameroons following the plebiscite, I became a member of the Cameroon National Union (CNU), the sole party created in 1966, which I served as president of the Mezam section. I stayed on as MP until my retirement from active politics in 1988. However, the launching of the SDF in Mankon and the dramatic resignation from the ruling CDPM in 1990 of John Ngu Foncha, brought me back to the centre of local and national politics. I was appointed to replace Foncha as the national vice-president of the CDPM. I fail to see why chiefs should be treated as apolitical animals or placed above party politics, when they are citizens just like anyone else. I have repeatedly challenged everyone to explain to me how a citizen can be deprived of involvement in politics simply because he holds a traditional title of Fon.

I didn't see how one can be so active in re-unification, politicking and seeking to convince the population about what options made sense, only for one to be disqualified from actively playing a role in the political life of the country following the plebiscite. This was especially questionable to my mind, since there was no regulation formally prohibiting Fons from seeking election into parliament. Worse still, I did not see that much thought had gone into the process of seeking to disallow Fons from running for parliament. I did not see what was prepared for the Fons to do instead. What was the part the Fons were supposed to play? I did not see the part the Fons were to play. So in that void I followed what was available. But it angered the political leaders and it started a 'black era' of seeking to turn my people against me, and of scattering my people.

That calls for my resignation as MP or Fon were politically motivated was clearly demonstrated when multiparty politics was abolished and the single party instituted. All of a sudden, the very same politicians and certain Fons who had urged that I resign saw little wrong co-opting Fons to serve within the party and run for parliament. Still when it came to me and Mankon, nothing was straight forward. Here again, if I did not query them, where would I be? They suppressed my opinion on national initiatives or issues involving my own people. However, since then and thanks to my tenacity, politicians began to see the wisdom of the Fon participating, joining them to administer the country politically. That is why I contested elections with the Fon of Bali who, previously, had opposed Fons doing politics, and had been so hostile to me becoming Member of Parliament. I defeated him and became section president of the CNU for Mezam Division. Why, one might ask, was the Fon found useful to serve as section president of the party – in the same way that I had been found useful to campaign for the plebiscite – yet considered to be 'dabbling into politics' or 'bringing Kingdom into disrepute' by seeking election into parliament? The only meaningful answer I can find when I ask myself questions like this is hatred – it was just hatred for me and my people. It seemed to be that both I and Mankon were being made to pay for the fact that I was an educated and enlightened Fon who saw in my parliamentary membership the best avenue of seeking recognition and representation for them and their interests at the highest level in our new and fast evolving dispensation as a country, nation or state.

It is worth mentioning that this idea of artificially divorcing Fons and politics was and remains a peculiarly Anglophone thing. At the same time that Foncha and the KNDP were persecuting me for going into politics, chiefs of the Francophone region were members of government, politicians and they had power. This was not something I introduced to Cameroon. For instance, Joseph Kamga of Bandjoun and many others were members of parliament, some members of government. Ibrahim Mboumbou Njoya who served as minister for long before succeeding his father to the throne in Foumban, has continued to be very active in politics at national level and in the highest instances of the governing CPDM party. Today, the

Prime Minister of Cameroon, Ephraim Inoni, is a chief. This, I believe, settles the quarrel between politicians and traditional rulers in this country.

Of course, most of the elites support the idea that I was a problem, because I opted to compete with them for elected office, and because I beat them to it. They tend to think that if I were out, they would have been ministers or taken my seat in parliament. I wouldn't want to name names, of people whom I have personally brought up or who have been assisted by me in the public service, but who write about me in such derogatory and accusatory a manner that could only be explained by bitterness that I must be having something they believe, rightly or wrongly, should be theirs. Some, even amongst the elite of Mankon, have allowed themselves to be influenced by such politics and politicians, oblivious of the real reasons why some parties are so hostile to Fons doing politics. They have supported those scheming to see me out of politics in the hope of being rewarded with sinecures, only for them to wait in vain, as neither the KNDP of the 1950s and 1960s nor the SDF of the 1990s and 2000s have shown they had anything to give them. On the contrary, the diversions and hesitation to subscribe to my vision and mission, has only resulted in their feeling manipulated with hindsight. Most of them today lament having been used and dumped by people whose commitment to change has seldom gone beyond the rhetoric of change. Instead of bringing about the end of suffering as their slogans have often suggested, both the KNDP and SDF have only, in reality, compounded the suffering of my people, determined as they have been, to plunder to oblivion the goodwill and generosity of spirit of the Mankon people.

Not only did the Mankon people massively support my first multiparty parliamentary term from 1962-1967, they also continued to back me up in subsequent elections into the unified parliament under the one party system of the CNU, and the CPDM from 1967-1988. Overall, I made five parliamentary terms over an uninterrupted span of 26 years from 1962-1988. As section president who managed the political affairs of the CNU at the divisional level, I also contested elections. In 1967 I successfully contested elections into the West Cameroon House of Assembly, where I later became deputy speaker. Finally the constitution of 1972, created only one parliament. I, again, was re-elected into the Cameroon National Assembly under the CNU from 1973-1983, and from 1983-1988 under the CPDM. When we returned to multipartyism in 1990, I was elected the First Vice Chairman of President Paul Biya's CPDM party, which I have been since then till now that I am celebrating my 50 years as Fo Mankon.

My political action during the 26 years was not limited only to parliamentary activities. I was also actively involved at the local level with contesting elections to occupy either seats of President of the Bamenda

Central Sub-Section or the President of the Mezam Section of the CNU and the CPDM parties. From 1967-1969, the Fon of Bali won the election to occupy the CNU Section President seat of Mezam. From 1969-1988, I repeatedly won the elections to occupy the Section President seat of the Mezam on both the platform of the CNU and the CPDM parties.

Whenever I did not personally contest the elections, I acted as adviser, and sometimes sponsored the candidature of some Mankon citizens for posts of section president as well as for other executive positions. It is most significant to state here that none of the political offices I contested and held during all of my political careers had a salary. It was only in parliament that parliamentarians were paid allowances or sitting fees.

It is worth reiterating that throughout my political career, I never only demanded political support from the Mankon people to support my candidature during elections, but also supported and campaigned for Mankon people to support the candidature of other Mankon citizens at political contests. The 1965 elections into the Federal House of Assembly in Yaounde were contested on a multiparty system in Cameroon, between the KNDP (of Hon. Dr Foncha) and the KNC (of late Dr E.M.L. Endeley) in the West Cameroon Federated State. Hon. D.A. Atia contested on the KNDP platform and indeed, I campaigned for massive vote for him in Mankon. In the 1988 parliamentary elections into the National Assembly of Cameroon, I again supported the candidature of Hon. D.A. Atia. Hon. S.A.A. Akenji who was voted into the National Assembly in the 1March 1992 parliamentary elections also received my support.

The benefits to Mankon of my active participation in politics have not only been increased political recognition and representation, but also greater socio-economic development. The developments are there for all to see, from the number of schools to medical services through businesses, pipe borne water projects and road infrastructure. There is the Congress Hall, the Airport, the motor parks, the Mankon Main Market, the Urban Council, the Mankon Museum, and many other development initiatives as testimony of my active involvement in politics in the interest of Mankon. It might not be as much as we would wish, but I have, since my childhood days, learnt to dream with my feet firmly on the ground. A bird at hand is worth two in the bush, was something I learnt as a school boy.

5

SDF the Reincarnation of KNDP

The Social Democratic Front (SDF) and the KNDP are one and the same thing, mirror images of each other. Not only is the SDF a rebirth of the KNDP, it was born in Foncha's house – there is no doubt about it. One party politics in Cameroon lasted from 1966 to 1990 when multiparty politics were re-introduced. The creation of the Social Democratic Front came with a return to the politics of the KNDP and the minimization of Mankon interests. This took the form of renewed rhetoric of the need for Fons to stay out of politics. Again, just like in 1961, I was the target, this time as First Vice Chairman of the CPDM, a position vacated when John Ngu Foncha resigned. Two years later, when there was a presidential election in October 1992, the SDF – a party I had allowed the freedom to establish itself and operate freely in my Kingdom, decided to target me, my property and the interest of the Mankon community for destruction. I didn't see any reason why after the re-introduction of multi-party politics within my Kingdom there could only be the CPDM and no other party, so I raised no objection to the creation and functioning of the SDF. I assisted in making them registered.

However, the SDF, like the KNDP of the 1950s and 1960s, had the impression that they were the party for the North West region, and anybody against them was a betrayal of the North West. And when I did not recline for SDF and they lost the elections to the CPDM, they started the interpretation that if I had joined the SDF, they would have won. Again, like the KNDP of old, they made of me their chief opponent and scapegoat. On October 23th and 24th, they conducted a malicious and violent campaign against me, through the wicked and unpatriotic act of contrivance, connivance and treachery of some Mankon citizens. They invaded, massively burnt, destroyed and looted my palatial premises and property in Mankon Urban. My traditional notables who supported me and who were administering Mankon tradition with me were also affected. Their homes were burnt down. The homes and premises of those Mankon citizens who have ever been elected to parliament (Hon. D.A. Atia, Hon. S.A.A. Akenji, H.R.H Fon Angwafo III) were burnt, property looted or destroyed. Young and old, elite and commoner who were inclining with my political views, were also targeted by SDF inspired violence. Their homes were burnt and their lives threatened. Alhadji Tita Fomukong, a Bali settler in Mankon who had founded his own political party – the CNP – was killed in Ngomgham. Most of the economic structures I had put up – the roads were tarred when I was Section President of the ruling party– most of them were destroyed. The markets were touched as well. That was the beginning of the Ghost Town operation and economic depression.

Thus, even though I was no longer Member of Parliament – having officially retired from parliament in 1988, even though I didn't contest the elections, the fact that I disagreed with a party that, all who had been against me in 1962 joined, everyone thought: 'Not again. He must be taught a lesson.' What I couldn't understand was the sudden about turn amongst the very same Mankon people – the elite, notables, clan heads, family heads and intellectuals especially – who had expressed appreciation, gratitude and congratulations through oral and written messages, individual and dance-group visits to the palace when I was elected member of the Central Committee and First Vice Chairman of the CPDM party (along with the Fons of Bali and Bafut who were elected as alternate members of the Central Committee). What could have happened barely three months after singing 'Te Deum' and 'Alleleuia' in appreciation of my election, for the very same Mankon people to engage themselves not only in agitating that I should resign that post of First Vice Chairman and quickly park myself out of active politics, but also to orchestrate a smear campaign of blackmail, calumny, defamation, misinformation and disinformation against the person of Fo Mankon amongst the people of Mankon? The answer lies in the SDF as a reincarnation of the KNDP, where a Mankon and the Mankon people were only relevant to the extent that they served others to achieve their ends. Mankon was presented and manipulated as a community not worthy of ambitions of its own, a community without self-interest, a community where strangers you have accommodated turn around to detect to you as if you were not the landlord.

Thus, if the SDF, like the KNDP its predecessor, could not suppress my political views, they could destroy my property, destroy my car, destroy the town and development I had fought for and made possible for the best part of 34 years as chairman of the Mankon Council from 1962 to 1996. Since the SDF took over control of the Council in 1996, they have never added anything to what I achieved for 34 years as chairman. All they have done is change the name from Mankon Council to Bamenda Urban Council, and brought in Nkwen and Mendankwe to be a wedge against Mankon progress. Initially, Foncha got Jomea Pefok from Bali, deputy permanent secretary in the Ministry of Local government during the KNDP administration, to come and be delegate, when they changed the Mankon Council into Bamenda Urban Council. Pefok served in that capacity from 1977 to 1992. Since 1992 when the Government delegate's position was passed onto Abel Nde Sanjou-Tadzong, a Mankon man, they are always quarrelling with him. Their decision to create councils for every other locality around Mankon, while denying Mankon the right to maintain its own council, in many ways holds back the progress of Mankon.

As the First Vice Chairman of the CPDM party, I accompanied the Head of State and national chairman of the CPDM, President Paul Biya, on a Common Wealth of Nations, Head of Government Summit, held at Auckland, New Zealand, on November 7 1995, following the admission of Cameroon into the Common Wealth of Nations, as the fifty-second member on November 1 1995. From John Fru Ndi's missions abroad as SDF chairman, his entourage over the years has hardly included Mankon delegates, despite the weight that some people in Mankon have thrown behind him and his party. So that he himself, he is not a Mankon, he is not from Mankon. There is no one from Mankon in his shadow cabinet either. I don't see Mankon there, which makes anyone wonder how much more Mankon has got to sacrifice for Mankon to be recognized and meaningfully represented within the SDF. John Fru Ndi and the SDF are acting from the very heart of Mankon, yet Mankon people remain invisible within the party. They are only visible when it comes to burning and destruction of their property. They are visible in making sacrifices for the party, but not in ripping rewards. This is why I see nothing but continuity between the SDF of today and the KNDP of old, when it comes to hostility and despising of Mankon. I have refused to accept such derogatory attitudes, and I have fought to preserve the dignity of Mankon for the past 50 years.

It was such marginalization of Mankon, even by strangers welcomed and accommodated on Mankon soil that made me particularly angry with sons and daughters of Mankon who gave them uncritical support, who signed a blank check for the SDF. My active participation in partisan politics from all these long years has been in total consonance with the prevailing policy of the incumbent Cameroonian governments. I therefore felt that if some Mankon people felt I had outlived my political usefulness and were disenchanted or disillusioned with my active involvement in partisan politics, for whatever reason – justified or unjustified – and would thus want to withdraw their political support, such feelings and messages should have been communicated to me and the Mankon notables directly. I felt bitter that instead of doing so, those Mankon people critical of my politics resorted to whispering campaigns of blackmail, slander and calumny. By so doing, they only played into the hands of opportunistic outsiders with ulterior motives that were only too ready to sponsor and magnify their smear campaigns of deformation and blackmail. Such opportunists readily exploited the political ignorance of the generality of the people and took advantage of the political naivety of the youth.

In Mankon we have always stood for construction against destruction, and for evolutionary change, which the Fons of Mankon have always spearheaded. So I was baffled to be accused of standing in the way of change, but, amongst others, Mankon some elite and youth, who saw that the only obstacle to change was the CPDM and those who supported it. I was labelled anti-change and requested to resign from the CPDM. My argument for refusing to yield was simple but firm. If such people requesting change were to eschew demagogy and prick their consciences, they would definitely acknowledge the fact that I have, during my 50 years on the throne, championed the course of meaningful cultural, economic and socio-political change and advancement in the Mankon Kingdom. I told them then, and would reiterate the same today, that I am a progressive and that I believe in change. I equally believe and attach great importance to change hinged on rational considerations and approach. Yes, I advocate change, and indeed join those clamouring for socio-political change in Cameroon, but the style, methodology and modality of bringing about such change is of paramount importance. Furthermore, I strongly advocate evolutionary change, and therefore, cannot and can never lend my support to any change, whatever the change, which is irrationally radical and motivated by a ruthless spirit of witch-hunting. My entry into active national politics and actions all these years was characterized by harmony and unity of purpose amongst the Mankon people. I should like to hand over the political relay baton to someone, rather than drop it to be picked.

For generations, Mankon has believed in construction, in life and in hope, and have organized themselves as a community around collective values. Communal work has always been part of Mankon tradition. The Europeans merely took advantage of it. Thanks to such dedication to work in the interest of the community, my father planned and realized the giant Mankon urban layout project in the early 1950s. By this, he succeeded in constructing the Commercial Avenue, the bye streets in Azire layout, as well as the main road linking Ntambag and the newly constructed Azire layout. Indeed, so committed to urban Mankon was my father that when the Sule – the Sarikin Hausawa of Abakwa who assisted the Fon as tax collector in urban Mankon – outlawed the selling of alcoholic drinks in Abakwa in 1950 on grounds that the women involved in the trade were untidy, and that the trade encouraged prostitution, my father felt insulted. He was equally insulted by a suggestion that, to curb crime, idlers in the township, who were mostly Mankon people who had drifted to the township in search of new opportunities, should be repatriated. Determined that the Sarkin had to be stopped, my father sent a delegation of educated Mankon notables – led by my elder brother Joseph Ndomu Fru-Asah, Nde Ntumazah, a court clerk, and Stephen Anye Awasom, a school teacher – to meet with the sarkin to convince him to consult with Fo Mankon before taking any major decisions with regard to Abakwa or the Mankon township, and to stop parading himself as a chief, because tradition did not allow the existence of two chiefs in one Kingdom.

In the light of these earlier developments and in view of similar ambitions of the time, the decision to change Mankon Council to Bamenda Urban Council, was clearly meant to divide Mankon into urban and rural, which was hardly the way I saw things. The urban council is my project since 1962 – I planned it, and building progressively, moving to urban setting. They say I am proud because I have the Urban centre, where economic activity is concentrated. But if they take a look back into history, they would notice that before independence in 1961, the town planning officers had studied the situation of the Bamenda area and proposed that we shouldn't have the government township. The officers had reached the conclusion that Nkwen could develop its own town, Mendankwe its own, and Mankon its own as well. Whilst I was busy developing Mankon town along the lines suggested, the others were doing little. And when they wanted to join me to develop the area, they came in with other motives – to deprive the bulk of Mankon people from the benefits of Mankon development by dividing them into urban and rural Mankon through renaming their council Bamenda Urban Council. However, I hope that the process of decentralization will come back to what it was before the Bamenda Urban Council – the development of separate Councils for Nkwen and Mendankwe, and the re-instatement of the erstwhile Mankon Council.

When I became Fo Mankon, I went to the Bamenda south west federation native authority with headquarters in Mbengwi to replace my father. The Divisional Officer in charge of the council lived at the station, and when we had council sessions he would come down, take me, and together we will go to Mbengwi. I objected to having the administrative headquarters of the council in a rural area while Mankon was urban. That brought me again a lot of friction with my colleagues. So I wanted a Mankon Council. My population was enough for me to have the council by local government regulations. John Ngu Foncha, who at the time was member in charge of local government, had to allow it on the provision that all other chiefs of the Ngemba speaking people should have a Ngemba Council and not a Mankon council. So that was what happened. They did everything to convince the other villages that I had a domineering population, and that if they all came together, the Mankon people will suppress them.

Foncha told them that Pinyin and Santa were much closer to them than Mankon and Mbengwi, with the sole purpose of dissuading them from allying with Mankon. He encouraged the other villages to join together, as the only way for them to fight Mankon.

So all the other villages met in Santa where they discussed the Ngemba Council. When we were to inaugurate it the first executive of that council, they drew up a list of councillors without my knowledge, and with the intention of keeping Mankon out of the executive. But somebody among them came down that same night of their secret meeting and informed me of what had taken place. We were to go to form the new council in the Mankon Community Hall the next day. So when I got the hint, I prepared myself, and went to the meeting with my own list, where I placed myself as chairman of the council and gave positions to other villages. Those who had met earlier in Santa did not know that I knew their plan, as they thought they had planned all behind my back. I had a big surprise for them. So when they started presenting their list, I objected on grounds that there was no councillor from Mankon on the executive. I then presented my own list, which took them quite by surprise, and my list was adopted. I became the chairman of the Ngemba Council and Member of Parliament as well. There was uneasy tension between Mankon people and the other villages. The fact that I defeated Nanga the KNDP candidate for the parliamentary elections of 1961, meant very difficult times for me and Mankon in the Ngemba Council, given the majority status of the KNDP in the area. So in 1961 things were not moving.

In 1962 the government wanted to make Mankon an urban centre like Douala. The tensions and conflicts threatened to derail the process. In 1964 we came to a compromise for a Mankon Town Council under a KNDP mayor and Fo Mankon as chairman. By 1968, as a Member of Parliament and chairman of the council, I was able to influence the reorganisation of the Ngemba Council, creating the Mankon Council for Lower Ngemba, and the Santa Council for Upper Ngemba. Of course, the Mankon people were very understanding, and were always in block when it came to elections, and whatever decision they took, whatever side they voted for won. This was a constant headache for Foncha, Christian Bongwa and others of the other villages who supported other candidates or alternative motions. The only way they thought they could beat Mankon was by deciding to transform the Mankon Town Council into the Bamenda Urban Council, that would alienate many other quarters of Mankon while bringing into the council Foncha's village of Nkwen and Bongwa's village of Mendankwe.

In that election again we were winning the election. When we became Bamenda Urban Council Jomea Pefok who had been elected the counsellor for Bali Council was appointed delegate for the Bamenda Urban Council and Pefok was the Deputy Secretary General in the Ministry of Local Government under one Mr Trot and responsible for all my problems from 1960 till then. Pefok knew everything – all the presentations, all petitions, all the antagonism between Mankon people and Foncha, and so Foncha used his position to get Pefok appointed as Government Delegate. Foncha was clearly expecting a fight, but I told the people that we shouldn't fight again. We should lie low and see whether this is the opportunity for him to take up the problem we had with the Bali people. My father had a land problem with the Bali people in 1952-1954. It was a fight to secure land for the wandering Ngen-mbu people. In 1962 Foncha had created a law targeted at Mankon as he sought to fulfil the land ambitions of villages and Kingdoms friendly to him and his KNDP. Suddenly, Nkwen people were claiming land between Mankon and Bali, alleging that they had a common boundary with the Bali people. The Nsongwa people were claiming they had land in Mankon, the Mendankwe people were saying their boundary with Mankon is the River Mezam. Everyone was claiming a piece of Mankon, and Foncha's 1962 law was meant to facilitate the task for them.

Then the time came when we wanted to build a council hall befitting the status of the urban council we had. Pefok, the government delegate, selected the site on which to build the council without consulting me. I don't know whether he had a special grant to build the hall, since as the chairman of the council I did not know. Wanki was the architect they chose for the project. He drew the plans. There was no approach to me, not even the courtesy of telling me what was happening. The council had no land and the council was, normally, to acquire land from Fo Mankon, but that approach was not done. They simply started work on the building. So at a council session, I asked to know who was building there. The architect brought the plans and tried to explain. I wanted to know who had authorised him to erect the building, what budget was financing the building that the chairman knew nothing about. How was the plot acquired without my knowledge as Fo Mankon and as chairman of council? Pefok acknowledged that the plot had not been acquired through Fo Mankon or the Mankon Traditional Authority. The project had not been passed at the session where we considered the estimates of the council. So we said, 'No, you have acted illegally. You have to explain.' Even the Governor tried to plead with us on behalf of Pefok, but we insisted. After several council sessions he resigned. He said he was sick, that somebody should take over. That was how Abel Nde Sanjou-Tadzong took over as Government Delegate. It is quite something that since Jomea Pefok resigned for health reasons, he never had fever all these years, until he passed away in July 2008.

After 50 years in politics and as Fo Mankon, I know I am crowned by successes. I have faced many challenges, especially from the KNPD in the early 1960s, and from the SDF in the early 1990s. But these storms I have weathered. Today, the fortunes of my detractors are declining, and the people of Mankon are all the wiser. I have been vindicated, because I have stood by my convictions all these years. I cannot see how the Fo is supposed to rule if he is forbidden active participation in politics. The Fo of Mankon was a ruler before partisan politics, and being Fo has always been a political office. I can't see how a good political arrangement could succeed in any set up where the Fo is excluded. The politics of the SDF, in this regard, is the same old politics of the KNDP, which I believe should have ended when I was elected into parliament as an independent, beating all the other candidates fielded by political parties.

I don't see what the Fo is supposed to do and what not to do. I feel that the Fo as a leader, as a legislator – traditional one – can continue to do that. It is up to government to clearly define the powers of the Fo, be these active or residual, but without ambiguity, so the Fo could continue with the business of administration. The struggle to abolish this and introduce that, based more on the sentiments of the moment than on any clear long term strategic plan, has done more harm than provided solutions to the burning question of the place of traditional authority in a modern state.

The easiest thing, I believe, is to rush into condemning our traditional systems of government. The real challenge is thinking things through in as cold headed manner, to ensure that we do not throw the baby of tradition out with the bathwater, in our desperate haste to embrace modern systems of power. We should study our traditional institutions side-by-side with the imported system we are trying to implement. We should see what is good in it, retain it, and support it grow. In this connection, I regret to say Foncha and the KNDP failed to do their work. We tried to form the House of Chiefs, it was closed – people closed their eyes. What other things did they do? What did they do? Nothing! They reduced the problem of traditional authorities to that of classification of chiefs. We were classified, but left without any measure of real powers as chiefs. Vaguely, they expected us to serve as auxiliaries of the administration, but that, in real terms, begs more questions than it has convincing answers. This was effectively a way of killing chieftaincy, yet expecting, in the same breathe, chiefs to exercise authority in favour of administrators and politicians.

If Fons are still relevant today beyond the tokenism of serving as auxiliaries, it is hardly thanks to the actions of politicians like John Ngu Foncha of the KNDP or John Fru Ndi of the SDF, who have been more interested in replacing or impersonating Fons by appropriating royal regalia and mannerisms. We have stayed relevant largely by taking things into our hands to mobilize and organize ourselves around matters of common interest to us Fons.

To maintain ourselves as embodiments of the particular cultural communities we head, we have had to dance to the tunes of changing times, constantly having to negotiate our positions within the contradictions between state and our communities on the one hand, and in relation to competing expectations within the communities on the other. Was it not Chinua Achebe, the Nigerian novelist whose books are well oiled by Igbo proverbs, who made a bird say, 'since men have learnt to shoot without missing, I have learnt to fly without perching'? Changing times for me and my colleagues have meant the ability to evaluate constantly and negotiate various innovations on the landscape of our politics and societies. We cannot afford to perch or rest on our laurels, lest we are swept away by the tides of change.

It strikes me as hypocritical for more and more of the same people who are so highly critical of Fons in modern politics, not to be satisfied with their achievements within the modern sector and bureaucratic state power. Increasingly, they come to us Fons seeking traditional titles of notability, with some ready to fight and kill for these titles. If chieftaincy was that incompatible with modern politics and bureaucratic state power, why then should they so desperately need recognition through traditional titles?

As more and more Fons and chiefs elsewhere have discovered their game, we have sought to beat them at it through mobilisation and organisation to defend our common interests. We don't always succeed, given the ability of the modern political elite to manipulate and divide in order to rule, but the fact that we can count some successes at all is a good sign that united we can indeed conquer. It was precisely to draw attention to ourselves a group of leaders with an important role to play in modern Cameroon, that we decided to honour President Paul Biya with the title of 'Fon of Fons' when he took over as head of state from Ahidjo in 1982. If the ritual meant that the President could benefit from our support as fellow Fons, it was also a message to him that he must do all in his powers to make us actively relevant to modern political processes.

Similarly, in 2000, we the Fons of the North West Province – which became the North West Region in November 2008, following a presidential decree transforming Cameroon's ten provinces into regions – once again collectively honoured Nico Halle, a prominent Douala-based lawyer from Awing in Bamenda, with the title of *'Ntumfo'* ('Fon's Messager'), in recognition of his distinguished contributions to the development of the North West region. To keep track of sons and daughters of our various Kingdoms, we Fons often appoint and install representatives among our subjects wherever there is a large enough community of our people. As 'sons and daughters of the soil' of Mankon for example, various urban elite in Yaounde, Douala, Limbe, Buea and all over the country have invited me to preside over ceremonies and functions aimed at enhancing their chances in the cities where they live and work. I, like other Fons, encourage cultural activities among urban migrants from Mankon, and am often called upon to inaugurate cultural halls built by MACUDA. Like similar other development associations, MACUDA is there to attract resources and opportunities for Mankon and Mankon people at home and abroad.

How could I, as Fo Mankon, not seek to maximise the best interests of the Mankon community? When this has meant seeking the best way of securing state protection in order to safeguard these interests in a context of keen competition for scarce resources and opportunities, I have never hesitated. Our politics since the days of the KNDP, has always been the politics of scratch my back I scratch your back. When I decided to run for parliament as an independent, it was because Mankon felt aggrieved that despite decades of scratching the backs of Foncha and other political leaders of the time, all it got in return was victimisation. And when Mankon was eventually recognised and represented thanks to my efforts, here the politicians came again with the reintroduction of multiparty politics in the 1990s, asking Mankon to sign blank cheques for John Fru Ndi and the SDF, without as much as promising anything in return. How could they expect to harvest where they hadn't sown? And how did they expect Mankon to sow where it was not sure to harvest?

Just like in the 1960s when Foncha convinced Fons to give the KNDP party their uncritical support, Fons who threw their weight behind Fru Ndi and the SDF in the 1990s, rapidly became disillusioned with unfulfilled promises. Like in the 1960s, they had been promised development in their home villages and revalorisation of their status. But when the opposition failed to win, the new political dispensation the Fons were hoping for failed to materialise. In supporting the opposition, disgruntled Fons were hoping for a new political dispensation that would reinstate the dignity of chieftaincy and reward them accordingly. No position in reality was politically neutral, even by those who, like Fon Fosi Yakumtaw (ex-provincial governor under the one party government since the time of Ahidjo), claimed that Fons should be above partisan politics. How could Fon Fosi Yakumtaw, who during his days as governor expected Fons to be actively involved in politics as auxiliaries of the administration, suddenly turn around to expect the very same Fons so schooled, to exercise neutrality in multi-party politics as a way of maintaining good relations with all political leaders?

The high point for the SDF and its illusions of popularity came at the 1996 municipal council elections where it won an absolute majority in 30 of the 32 councils in the then North West Province. It also picked up a few urban councils in other parts of the country, but their greatest gains were here. However, since then, the political fortunes of the SDF have dwindled, and with that dwindling of political fortunes corresponds a dwindling number of Fons openly in support of the opposition or the neutrality of chiefs in partisan politics. Since the amendment of the constitution to protect ethnic and regional minorities politically in 1996, we Fons of the North West have mobilised ourselves under various lobbies to demand more recognition and resources from government, often in opposition to the competing interests of our counterparts within and in other regions. In general, we are conciliatory to the ruling party and government as the finger that feeds or could feed us and our Kingdoms. We would like to see the House of Chiefs abolished in 1972 in favour of the unitary reinstated. We are encouraged by the 1996 constitutional reform that provided for a senate, to which the head of state is entitled to appoint half of the members. Although there is fierce competition and rivalry amongst us for power and resources from the centre to our various regions and Kingdoms, we are very conscious of the fact that even such individual aspirations are best achieved only through mobilisation and organisation, and above all, through being conciliatory with the state.

We have thus come up with associations such as the North West *Fons'* Union (NOWEFU), networks and other forums that enable us collectively to stake claims on national power and resources for our region and Kingdoms. Since no Fon intends to conquer another, there is no reason why we shouldn't unite to confront common problems. If Fons have a common problem, in the union we present it to government and the Fons have a common advantage from that union. So even if we are in factions it's the same problem we are putting, it's the same duty we are rendering to the people and in the course of that we have the same experience. It is all these experiences, responsibilities and claims on our leadership as Fon, which I fail to see why Fons should be treated as apolitical animals or placed above party politics, when they are citizens just like anyone else. How can you deprive a citizen of involvement in politics simply because he holds a traditional title of Fon?'That's the unanswered question, as far as I am concerned.

If I have stood firm up to this day, and all the traditional leaders who initially distanced themselves and were critical of my stance, have now followed my way, that to me is a great achievement. The Fons, some of them my age group, who were attacking me are now with me, doing exactly what they accused me of doing, that to me is an achievement – my tenacity, staying firmly committed to what I believed to be right, despite the pressure and criticism. I refused to waver. I kept my direction.

I think that we have evolved. There have been a lot of changes since the British left us. Societies have changed from what we used to know them. Not least are the changes that have taken place in chieftaincy as an institution. I however believe that chieftaincy remains a relevant force in rallying or mobilising the population for self-help initiatives. There have been changes in literacy standards and we have done a lot of mixing. We got independence by signing to unite with the Cameroon people east of the Mongo, which we believed to be the right thing to do. Other countries like Germany have since followed our example by reuniting after decades of living asunder as if not one and the same people. Today, Europe is unifying governments, and its peoples are forming the European Union. The idea of unification is now worldwide. Even Africa now has the African Union.

At first view, these worldwide unifications and movements towards large-scale communities might mean the end of our kingdoms. But, on a closer look, it makes these kingdoms even more relevant, as big unions can only function to the extent that they are well grounded in the various localities which constitute them. It is true that the modern laws which conflict with the old traditional laws weaken the original stamp of authority of the Fons. But our kingdoms and modern law makers like parliament where I served for over 25 years before my retirement in 1988, have proved their dynamism in their ability to listen and make concessions in the interest of progress. There is therefore no reason for the state to fear Fons, and for Fons to be uncomfortable with the state. In the same way, there is no reason for the educated elite to be afraid of Fons or to feel comfortable only when dealing with illiterate Fons they can easily pocket or manipulate. If we really are committed to development, I believe there should be room enough in this aspiration for everyone to play a part.

So, I believe that if chieftaincy were recognised as an administrative unit, with the jurisdiction of each Fon coinciding with a subdivision or division, we would have made more progress. If a subdivision was a kingdom, if a division was a kingdom, we would have made more progress. You know the human being each man want something for himself, he wants to labour for himself or for his children. When you have posted administrators they come like that, they look like intruders and so maybe we started with the politicians, the politicians were commoners. Politicians were children to the rejected parents. Princes and princesses, it was a taboo for them to go to school and carry water for the Headmaster or to be flogged. My fathers, they couldn't have gone to school. Their royal or princely dignity did not allow them to embrace what in their eyes was beneath royalty. So, for foolish reasons, they gave out the chances that came their way, and most of the people who went to school were Nchindas.

This means that, as many of our rulers, our politicians are people who have learned the art of government from Europeans or from foreign countries, and not their own cultures and traditions. If the government were to know the differences and study or research the customs, traditional laws and customs of the various kingdoms, they would find that there is nothing bad in this institution and we would have made more progress. We would achieve more progress even in the development of the education and the development of the kingdoms.

As I'm saying since 1960 I have all these struggles worrying me and that God has still preserved my life. I'm sure that after my death, those who compile my balance sheet shall note that I never wavered from my agriculture. That I had had the advantage of going to parliament, making laws, debating laws, understanding the law and being able to sift what traditionally is wrong, and applying my decisions with the knowledge of the law.

6

Churches, Schools and Politics

The role of the church in politics is very evident, when one takes a closer look at John Ngu Foncha and his KNDP party, and John Fru Ndi and his SDF respectively. The church is also a type of political organization. For instance, when Foncha was Headmaster of RCM School Mankon, there were local teachers with him. But when Foncha became Prime Minister, he didn't want to see any Mankon man, even the Catholics. Many teachers were appointed D.Os, but not a single one of that was Mankon. In some cases, those he appointed D.Os, weren't the match of some people like Ndi Fomabad – that was a more serious, superior teacher. But you had Gamndje, you had Epo, you had so many of the Catholics there, but no one Mankon.

The churches may have preached about one God, but they did not always agree. The trouble between Catholics and Presbyterians featured when I was in Parliament. When Foncha left for Yaounde as the Vice President of the Republic, he had recommended Muna to Ahidjo as the person to take over from him as Prime Minister of West Cameroon. He had told Ahidjo that he knew Muna well and that Muna was a good man. But when Foncha returned to West Cameroon and consulted with the bishop, he tried to shift to a Catholic Prime Minister, having received objections from his church circles to the fact that Muna was a Presbyterian. The bishop had complained that Muna being a Presbyterian might stand in the way of the Catholic ambition to open new schools and build missions and health centres here and there, as a way of staking claim to vast and strategic portions of land all over West Cameroon. The fear of the Catholics was that Muna would prefer and facilitate the opening of Presbyterian schools and missions instead. And so Foncha tried to change to introduce Augustine Ngom Jua, a Catholic, as prime minister.

Thus began the conflict of the churches, religious confrontations in politics. The churches were fighting for influence, first the setting up of schools, then the church will follow. That was especially the Catholic programme. Foncha, as a Catholic, was expected to have known and defended Catholic interests in the appointment of a prime minister to replace him in West Cameroon. He didn't have to wait for them to tell him. And so when he surrendered the premiership to a Presbyterian, they were terribly disappointed. In fact, the death of multiparty politics after independence to give rise to the CNU in 1966, was a church affair. It was soon after that that Muna started his own CUC, immediately endearing himself with Ahidjo who thought that KNDP and Endeley's party were a problem to him. The creation of the CUC also propelled Ahidjo to act fast to institute the one party regime, as a pre-emptive measure against further splits in the major parties in West Cameroon. It was also possible, Ahidjo believed, that the disease of splitting parties will spread over to East of the Mungo, and he quickly manoeuvred to create the one party. In this project, he was significantly assisted by the churches, albeit indirectly, through the conflicts and scheming to position Christians of their denominations in key positions of power and influence.

The situation in the 1990s with the coming of the SDF was not dissimilar. It isn't so much that Fru Ndi knows politics or that he knows anything, but that he is bold, he is able to challenge – that is his qualification. Even if John Fru Ndi is not Catholic, the fact that his party is an incarnation of John Ngu Foncha's KNDP, means that he was consciously made to defend Catholic interests.

As a child growing up in the palace, we were exposed to all the religions, because there was not a Christian denomination that did not visit my father, talking to him, seeking to convert him and so on. But it was the Catholics who really wanted to have a second school to Sasse, up here. I seized that opportunity. I didn't specially want a Catholic school. All I wanted was a secondary school near enough to accommodate the Mankon children I wanted educated. Nigeria was too far away. I had had the experience of schooling in Nigeria, and didn't see any Mankon man who could pay transport and keep his children far away in Nigeria. Throughout my stay in Nigeria, I didn't see anything, any Bamenda man there. So, I knew it would be very good if I had a secondary school, so poor parents could afford to send their children to school. I thus saw the approach by the Catholics to open a college as an opportunity for me to attract the school to my own land. I didn't propose the idea. Same for the Basel Mission!

What really moved me were the Baptists! I made the approach to the Baptists. I was drawn to them because in 1960, they had a Baptist missionary here who was a very good and influential man. He used to visit me – we talked politics, talked sociology, talked anthropology, and he could go to South Africa, and bring me books. I have most of my library from him, and he had quite a big influence in the region, especially in the Nkambe area. I enjoyed his approach to religion – he helped, he kept speaking. He was here in Nkwen and built many schools there. I had to approach him for a primary school, and he built the school at Musang. I tried to make use of all the missionary bodies. The Presbyterians wanted a teacher training institution, so I provided land for them as well. Now the Catholic and Presbyterians had secondary school each, I saw the religious conflict, dragging the people here and there. I attracted the Baptist, gave them land for the Baptist high school. I consider education the major thing, if its religion, okay – the Bible is one so let all of them be talking their religion. And I believe that, in as much as my children, my population belongs to all these, I think I embrace all the religions. I belong to all or to none. So, I didn't want any political friction. And of course, I think it also solves the problems, because at the time of the Catholics and the Basel, they never talked to each other. Once a Catholic, he had nothing to do with a relative who is a Basel. Today, they don't see the difference. Today they can even inter-marry.

Mankon has been most generous to the Churches. Not only have we welcomed the various missions to set up schools and build churches, we have embraced all of them within the community and even in the palace. I have already mentioned how my elder brother and I attracted the wrath of our father for daring to marry in a Catholic Church in my brother's case, or move from a government to a mission school, in my case. As I have also indicated, it wasn't so much that my father was against Christianity, but rather than he disapproved of their principles of one man, one wife. His open door policy toward strangers and other ways of seeing and doing included opening up to the churches in everything but their idea of marriage. I have been even more conciliatory. Not only have I allowed my wives and children to go to the churches of their choice and attend mission and government schools indiscriminately, I have even allowed my children to wed in church.

1985 was the year I first conceded to and attended a church wedding since succeeding my father in 1959. One of my sons, Ephraim Nde Ngwafo, then law lecturer at the University of Yaounde where he later became professor and Rector, was marrying a woman from Manyu Division. Ephraim was also one of the few of the young generation of princes not only to choose his wife from outside of Mankon, but to venture out of the North West Region. He had grown up in the South West Region where his father had migrated, and knew more of South West and South Westerners than of the North West. In addition, he had left Cameroon to study abroad in London and Dalhousie where he earned his PhD in law. The wedding took place at the Saint Joseph's Metropolitan Cathedral in Mankon.

Shortly after Ephraim's wedding, his brother, Fru Asanji – a urologist who had lived in the USA for over 20 years – married in the United States without my blessings, to Charmaine, a woman from the Caribbean. Although ready to allow for marriage to someone from outside of

Mankon, I was not yet ready to concede to marriage with someone as far away as America. So I was not happy with what Asanji had done, not because I didn't like his wife, but because of the idea of proximity in choosing a partner for marriage I had grown up knowing. But as time passed and Asanji explained his position, I finally understood him and yielded to the marriage eventually, on one condition: that Asanji returned to Mankon with his wife and that he underwent the traditional marriage ceremony as well. Asanji now lives and works in Yaounde, where he is Secretary General at the Ministry of Health, and professor of Medicine with the University of Yaounde School of Medicine, CUSS. Together with Ephraim, Asanji is also a key adviser to me. Following this precedence, another of my sons, Cletus Nde Tamukum, who went to the USA for further studies married Sherry, an African-American as well, and in 1999 came home briefly to present his wife and son to the family in Mankon, and to undergo some traditional rites too.

These traditional rites were important in that they transformed both marriages from a contract between two individuals (*usa'mangyie*) to marriage by consensus (*ngoo manyie*). The traditional rites entail anointing the groom and bride with powdered cam wood and red palm oil, and pouring a drink of raffia wine from my drinking buffalo-horn into their hands scooped around their mouths to avoid spillage. The anointment blesses them with fertility, and the wine transmits to them some of my life essence as father, thus taking away their symbolic impotency. This buffalo-horn cup which I inherited from my father, I am going to bequeath to whoever succeeds me as Fo Mankon. This cup makes of me not only father to my immediate family, but also father to all, entitled to pour libation on the graves of dead Fons and ask for blessings and protection on behalf of everyone in the Kingdom of Mankon.

Thus, having allowed for a church wedding in 1985, I needed no further convincing when it came to the turn of Francis Nyamnjoh in December 1990, who married the daughter of a local notable from Ntambeng. It was a more traditional wedding than the others in that once he had made known his intentions to marry Mambo, I as wife-taker started negotiations with her family as wife-giver when Nyamnjoh was still in the UK studying for his PhD. I completed payment of the bride wealth long before Nyamnjoh returned home. The marriage started with the traditional rites as described above, which I performed in person at the palace. Another rite (*miy*) was also performed to prove that Nyamnjoh had qualified to wear shoes into the inner-courtyard of the palace where I grant daily audiences, and that he could thenceforth greet or speak directly to the Fon and could attract the Fon's attention by clapping his hands; all things he was not allowed to do until 1990. Nyamnjoh had come of age. Ambroise

Ngang Ngu, his family in law, satisfied with the bride wealth, officially handed their daughter over to us, and considered her married. As was the custom, Mambo was led to the palace at night by a singing group of her relatives with bamboo lights (*nka*). None of her kin was happy to be separating from her, although they all shared her joy at marriage. The idea of night and bamboo light is intended to discourage the bride from rushing back to her parents each time she has a dispute with her husband, even as she pays regular visits to her parents.

Ten years later was Vincent Adebang's wedding, on January 8 2000, at the Presbyterian Church Ntamulung in Mankon. Adebang wanted to crown his PhD in Engineering by getting married, and, like for his brothers above, I entered negotiations with the family of his chosen bride as a wife-taker. The wife was the daughter of Solomon Forgwe, a former vice-minister of agriculture and reverend pastor of the Baptist Church in Cameroon. They were based in the UK and USA respectively, and had both decided to come home for their traditional, civil and church weddings. This accomplished, they both returned to the USA where the bride was employed and the groom was hoping to find a job. Many more marriages have followed, by sons and daughters based at home and abroad, and of all walks of life.

In these and other marriages I have conducted locally, I am also actively involved and represented at the next stage - that of the civil marriage, which is performed by the Government Delegate of the Bamenda Urban Council. This stage is important, for the Delegate issues a marriage certificate which the state recognises, and in which the man has the choice of indicating whether he opts for polygamy or monogamy. The churches insist on this stage and on seeing what option the groom has settled for before deciding whether to allow for a church wedding as well or not. Those who opt for polygamy have their applications for a church wedding turned down, since the church, unlike the state, allows only for monogamy. An increasing number of couples settle for this stage only.

I am as involved as a wife giver as I am as a wife taker. On June 20 1998, my daughter, Doris Manka – professional secretary in a bank in Yaounde – married a magistrate Joseph Aseh Malego, prince from the Kingdom of Balikumbat. This wedding was attended by 8 other Fons, who were keen to display their solidarity as members of our union of Fons. Also in attendance was the Governor of the North West Province, as a close administrative collaborator. The pattern was the same as for the previous weddings, but since this was a daughter's wedding, I as wife-giver was expected to personally hand Doris over to the husband in church, the same way that her brothers and sisters had escorted her to the groom's home a few days back. I led her up to the altar in church, and commenting on the wedding later I said: 'It is her choice and I grant her that. If she has saved enough to finance it, I'll encourage her to go ahead.' Many other marriages – including most recently those of Julius Tsi, Linda Nanga, Loveline Agwara, and Kennedy Ntsewah – have taken place, all involving the traditional, most going to the civil stage, and some going all the way to the church. Sometimes it is the Catholic Church, sometimes Presbyterian, and sometimes Baptist. But whatever the church, I, as a non-denominational Christian and wife giver or taker, am there to see my children through.

Not only have my sons and daughters married in church and in court after the traditional rites in the palace, some of them have married into other Kingdoms. My daughter, Rose Ngum, is married to the Fon of Babungo. Oscar Tse Tamandom is married from the palace of the Fon of Oku. These marriages not only link the two royal families, they bring together and strengthen ties between the people of Mankon and these other Kingdoms. The Fons have a say in my palace just as I have a say in their palaces, through marriage.

To me, education is the key to any meaningful achievement. I have known this since the day I first set foot in school. I have encouraged my children to get as much of it as possible, and have prioritized it despite the many other challenges demanding a share of our meagre resources. Although education necessarily comes with new values, I believe that a thorough grounding in our own ways best prepares us to adapt the values we adopt through education.

I have insisted more on the citizens who are my children to get an education. My contribution to illiteracy eradication since I became Fo Mankon, has been informed by the difficulties we went through struggling to get educated in our days. I have never thought that anybody could suffer the way I suffered to have my secondary education, because the very first day I left here and entered Mamfe in a Canoe, trekked to Nigeria in 11 days. I had never seen a canoe before in my life. It was a challenging experience, yet I managed to have come out safely. I couldn't see any young man of my age going through the same trial. The only other person I know was George Kisob, who would have had the support of his uncle. This explains why when the Catholics wanted to open a secondary school like Sasse up in these parts, I couldn't let the opportunity pass me by. Initially, they planned to site the college at Banso, but I intervened. I protested that, 'You cannot make Mankon headquarters with a future, with all the Reverend Fathers here and then you jump Mankon. The Sacred Heart College must be built here.' When they complained that there was no land, I showed them land, my hunting ground in Ngomgham, and challenged them to add the palace to it if the land was not enough. So the matter was settled.

When the Presbyterians wanted to build a teacher training centre, they started it in Bafut. I attracted them here. They built their Women's Teachers

Training College which they later converted to Presbyterian Secondary School at Atua-kom Mankon. Then I attracted the Baptist to build Baptist High School Mankon on the hill at Matsam. I encouraged the Longlas and Victor Asobo who abdicated as Chief of Pinyin to build a secondary school in Mankon. I provided land for Our Lady of Lourdes College and so on. So I have several schools, mixed schools, boys' schools, schools specially for girls, schools built by government, government colleges, and then private colleges, missionary colleges within my Kingdom. I am pleased that thanks to these efforts, there are primary and secondary schools enough for Mankon children and for children from elsewhere to assist me in the fight against illiteracy. I have solved a problem, the problem that no child shall ever again be subjected to the suffering I went through in quest of education.

When we gave land to the Catholics, Presbyterians and the other missions, they paid tribute to the palace, not in terms of gifts but in terms of recognition of the Fon's symbolic authority as landlord. But government now makes it possible for them to register land directly, thus giving them the power to run counter to the Fon. Thus once the land that was given the missions free of charge and as a sign of Mankon's commitment to education and development is registered directly by the missions in their name, Mankon loses the special relationship and recognition in tribute that the missions had with it as landlord. There is need for this particular relationship to be revisited. Land not being infinite, it fails to make sense that institutions to which the people of Mankon generously donate land should consider this land their private property and proceed to register it as such. This is a matter for Fons to take up in future reflections, and explore ways by which Fons could continue to serve on boards of schools or whatever institutions are erected by missions on land given them by Fons. Such representation should be on a permanent basis to cater for the interest of the cultural community where they are settled. Failing this, one could envisage a future when the chiefs just become symbolic authorities instead of cultural authorities where they are relevant to the point that people think there are sacrifices to be made.

The reverend father is a business man now you cannot say that he is not. So is the pastor. They have admitted that they are in business. So instead of continuing to deal with them as if they were just out for the interest of the poor, I now tell them we must agree on terms before they occupy whatever land they are interested in me giving them as landlord. I've told the church I've given enough land and now they are rich enough even to buy land.

Those of them who insist on a land certificate I tell them, while we do not oppose the idea of a land certificate, by the Mankon custom royal land cannot have a certificate because the tradition is on handing down to the next generation and Fon as custodian of culture and landlord. So to have a certificate means at one stage all the land is going to be given over and there will be nothing to hand. Also if somebody has applied for a land certificate, I say your father was given that land with the duty of providing drinks to the palace, bringing food and so on. For a long time we have not received wine from your bush. How do I feed the people even for rituals only? Where do I get goats and fowls for sacrificial purposes? So people can have their land certificate, but not on royal land.

Royal lands currently controlled by individuals, families or clans are given them in trust. We have an agreement with them to the effect that the land is for them to harness, and not to own. Often, the time comes when the government wants land for this or that project, and turns to me to provide it. I should be able to determine which of the lands currently in trust with this or that person or village, is best suited for the project at hand. It is not easy for the government to know otherwise, but it is on this basis that we have functioned. To ask us to stop this system of land management implies that they want us to stop chieftaincy, which is tantamount to destroying our cultural heritage. That is why we are authorising people to own their land certificates but those authorised to farm or tap mimbo on royal land they are barred from having land certificates.

I think the main problem is that of an idea of democracy that is articulated around the empowerment of the individual, forgetting that there is a democracy that requires the empowerment of the community whose interests are superior to those of the individual. That is why I tell my children, each and every one of them, if you don't find me tomorrow the next Fon must have several wives. It's a community you are serving, and not the individual. When I came here 50 years ago, I had no intention of staying. Being Fo Mankon did not interest me. But as I listened to the king makers, my mothers and others echo the will of my father, I decided that the collective interests were more important than my comforts as an individual. In the same way, I am going to hand the people and the land to the next Fo Mankon and so it should go from generation onto generations. If it comes to a time when the office or institution of Fo Mankon is handed to a successor with no land, that shall be the end of a collectivity as we have known and lived it. Our ability to negotiate as a collectivity is tied to a certain authority over land. Individual claims to land make sense only to the extent that the moral authority of the landlord as a community is respected. It thus becomes dangerous to imbue individuals with rights and entitlements to land without making them understand their responsibilities over that land as a cultural resource that is meant to be used judiciously and not abused, and always in the interest of the collectivity. The future of our communities as cultures is certainly jeopardised by the indiscriminate parcelling out of land to individuals and the feeling that creates that land certificates can overwrite cultural histories of special relationship between communities and their land. It is for democracy to recognise in principle and practice the rights of cultural communities which are Kingdoms, kingdoms of various kinds and then to see to what extent there is a balance between them.

It is a fact that religion plays a part in chieftaincy and in politics. When Muna was to take over from Foncha, the friction between Muna and Jua was more or less a friction between the Catholics and the Presbyterians and so when we talk about the people divided into political parties we have not exposed the real division which is among the churches. Another matter where the church plays a political role is in the transformation or stigmatisation of the many good customs in the traditions of our people. What is traditional and appreciated by our people the church considers bad not because of any legal or for any human reason, but because of the Bible and its preaching.

For instance, perhaps I could have done more if I had only one wife here. But imagine myself to have inherited more than seventy wives from my father to add to my own under that pressure. For one man to have hundreds of children to raise them up, it's been thanks to God that we are managing and it may appear that we may win. Just about twenty of my children are left for me to take care of now so in another five or ten years I may be free.

People give the Fon as many wives as he wants but the deterrent is your ability to raise the children properly. If the future should be any brighter, the degree of our understanding is easier when the population is literate. The ability of the Fon to guide his people also depends on his education and training, not on the number. To be able to have somebody who can play that role you need three or four wives, because if you have only one wife and she happens not to have a son, or one that can make a Fon, then that's the end of it. If you have to make a selection you imagine it should be a selection from a number, which means ensuring that you have enough to select from. You cannot select from one woman alone. So I think what divides the Fons more is the government because some of the Fons become beggars. Some of the Fons cannot live on their own. Some of the Fons cannot even command their people. Some will submit to other Fons, sell their own ranking because they cannot defend it. But with a good education enough for them to earn a living, Fons do not wait for other people to support them. Also, we expect that Fons have acquired over the years the status of being landlords or managers of the land, even when they give them to churches for purposes of education or to hospitals. But given that land is not infinite and that the regime of land management recognises the Fon to the point where they decide on ownership and attribution of land once it's signed out it becomes an individual, writing Fons into the long term future of their communities as landlords and managers would be a good way of reconstituting and guaranteeing the power of Fons in the long run.

Even then, having a large family is hardly a problem as such, even if I agree it is a formidable challenge, especially these days. The advantages of large families were much more evident in those days of my father and forefathers. During warfare, the defence of the village came from your womb or from your village. Today, it is a little less obvious, but the needs for defence are still relevant, even if the type of warfare has changed remarkably. We need many children if our responsibilities are many, so as to have an educated troop of soldiers – hundreds of them, well educated and seeking to position themselves as soldier, gendarmes or policemen, and in other professions, so that they could all contribute their fair share of your earnings to the collective project of uplifting the family and community to a better life. So the wars we fight these days are to ensure that each and every child attain the heights they aspire to attain as educated youths, so that they in turn could revamp the voluntary payment of tributaries, the obligatory form of which I abolished in 1960.

Thanks to my option for agriculture, I now feed the people instead of the people feeding me as wont. So, from the point of view of my responsibilities vis-à-vis the wider family and the Mankon community, chieftaincy does not allow for monogamy, even if I would say that in the time of my father, polygamy was overdone. Three to five wives may be good for the Fon, and twenty or so children okay. With such a modest number, the Fon could give them reasonable education. But in my case, and indeed, in the case of many Fons I know, Fons have been left on their own to fend for themselves by populations who continue to look up to Fons and chieftaincy as a custodian of culture and traditions and dispenser of basic administration. What the Fons are able to do administratively with regard to the needs of their populations, no ordinary civic administrator can. The local administrator, however gifted and trained and well-intentioned, simply cannot do what the Fons do. They don't know how to, because to solve a problem you have to understand the culture and traditions of the people posing or experiencing that problem. Decisions cannot be imposed. Well intended as these may be, the laws of the modern state do not command the same sense of appreciation as the customary laws that draw on and are inspired by the traditions and customs of those seeking judgement on problems that derive from and pertain to their traditions and world views.

7

Building the Palace, Tending the Kingdom

I'm a farmer even at my age. I'm farming so nobody should think that it is a disgrace to farm. Whether you are a governor, a member of parliament or you are a Fon, we are responsible for our future and so everybody should try to work hard and, of course, all my children owe me a debt. If I've helped my daughter or son to acquire education, it is his or her responsibility to educate their own son or daughter. I'm not educating the children because I have the means. Rather, I do it because I must. So we have to sacrifice to realise our objectives as a family and as a people. Our salvation is in the soil, both literally and metaphorically. With this spirit, the future is clearly a bright one for all and sundry in Mankon.

On March 13 1973, I was decorated as officer of Cameroon Agricultural Order of Merit, and on May 20 2000, I was raised to Commander of Agricultural Order of Merit by the Cameroon government. I have had several other awards and recognitions in my life, but these two, together with the recognition I have gained from my very own people in the field of agriculture, stand tall and have a special place in my heart.

I grew up gardening, and was trained to be an agriculturalist. I worked in that capacity in Menchum and other Divisions. When I was enthroned Fo Mankon, I didn't abandon my job as an agriculturalist. To me, becoming Fo Mankon was like transferring me to continue with agriculture in Mankon. So I have continued with agricultural activities, because I trained to be an agriculturalist. I have stayed in agriculture both for the income it brings, but also to continue demonstrating several aspects of the sector with the hope that some people might find it valid, especially given the high rate of unemployment in the country. For 50 years of staying faithful to agriculture, I don't think I have failed in that. I was raised thanks to agriculture. I went to school thanks to agriculture. I stayed in school and graduated into a job thanks to agriculture. If I have subsisted as Fo Mankon, send my children to school, attended to the health needs of my family, and brought a smile of hope on the faces of Mankon people and those strangers we've accommodated in Ntambag, it is thanks to a commitment to agriculture.

Happily enough, my people do not object to my still continuing agricultural work. What is the Fon suppose to do or not do for himself, for his children? What are the people supposed to do for the Fon in order to let him steer towards what he is asked to do, and yet manage the lives as the father, a married man with his family, who takes care of them? And the palace, building and maintaining the palace, who is supposed to do it? Traditionally, many people are silent over these questions, but how we answer them would determine what we want to make of those on whose shoulders we place the responsibility of the institution of Fo Mankon.

In the past, it was easy to say building the palace was the responsibility of the people. But given the evolution we have gone and are still going through, how easy is it for ordinary folks in the quarters of Mankon to build the palace? Where do they get the blocks, the panes, the zinc – all resources that are not local. These are not natural resources. They cannot be harvested from the forests or hills in the same way that was possible to harvest trees, bamboos and grass in the days of Ndefru III or Angwafo II. While these ordinary folks are ready to assume their responsibilities vis-à-vis the palace, modern building facilities have evolved beyond their determination to be relevant. They don't have the money to pay for these things. All they have is their commitment to their culture and traditions. So who has taken care of me? Apart from the need to safeguard our cultural practices, arts and values, the tradition is silent over many things, not least of which is the lifestyle of the Fon. Who is taking care of the Fon? What are the implications of letting the Fon take care of himself? These are weighty questions that must be answered, as the answers we give them determine the type of Kingdom and Fon we want, and consequently, how well we are able to consolidate and renew our culture and traditions.

With no convincing answers to these questions forthcoming, I thought the best way was to practice agriculture, what I knew best, a dependable ally since my childhood days. Thanks to agriculture, I have been able to provide for the family and assist widows and orphans, which traditionally is the role of the Fon, even if the community has not exactly made any provision for that. In Mankon we say that the Fon is the father of all widows and orphans, but what is given the Fon to ensure that he performs this role with distinction?

People bring to me and daily remind me of things the Fon should do for them and for Mankon. Most of the challenges they face are addressed to me. What are the people doing as their responsibility to the Fon? Before becoming Fo Mankon, I didn't know anything about these mutual responsibilities. Now I know what the responsibilities are. Until you wear the shoe, you can't say where it pinches. I think each Fon in his own time has a contribution to make. I have worked hard towards independence, visibility and representation for Mankon at the local and national levels, and why not at the global level as well? But others, like Foncha and Fru

Ndi have tried to break the Mankon and its community into pieces. What these experiences and trying times have thought us is that we can only achieve lasting progress when we consider and pursue it as a collective cause. Because I, like my father and forefathers, have always fought for the collective dignity and interests of Mankon, those who have opposed me, like those who opposed my father and grandfather, have remained miserable. But the fact of being eternally forgiving, of preferring a united to a divided Mankon, means that there is always room to welcome back to the fold the repentant prodigal son.

I am proud because I have a council. I wasn't given a town – the council I created. So, although the administration and politicians have interfered in a way, we have always been proud of the community work we've done since the time of my father, to construct the town, from Old Town to the New Town, which was bush. We transformed Mankon into an urban commercial centre – with trade, commerce, industry, and so on. I have a love for farming. But my love for farming means that I have to stay in the village, but that does not make the town any less Mankon. Before my rest house in Ntambag was targeted and burnt down by the SDF opposition in 1992, that was where I used to stay when I wanted to receive people and attend to matters in town. The interference by hostile politicians who do not mean well for Mankon, has delayed our plans and ambitions for Mankon. Due to such diversions, the town planning started by my father in 1954 has not been followed up as well as I would have liked. If they had allowed me to pursue the vision the way I started, it is easy to build good roads and install facilities such as water, electricity at cheaper cost to me. But when they scatter the population and so on, the costs are high and that's why they have not achieved much for Mankon ever since they took over the council.

In any case, I am determined to forge on with my development efforts, detractors notwithstanding. I have been creating centres where I intend to woo the population to. For instance, I went to Yaounde and demanded the technical school, and we were granted one at Ala-Bukam. We received quite good collaboration from the Mankon elites and were able to put up the structures for Forms One and Two to have the school officially launched. All the people who have compounds there, they have water, they have electricity, they have their health centre, they have their school, they have their market. Life will be easier, and administration will be more effective. These are ideas I am selling. I have strategic points in preparation for the population to attend to their needs and make a difference in their lives. I provide spare land for cultivation. Land is central to everything, and I call on all Mankon people to use it judiciously and efficiently. What we do or don't do with land is central to what we are able to achieve. We must use land in such a way to ensure that we have land for the coming generation for building, for their food needs, small stock farms and so on. So I am satisfied with these initiatives and hope that every son and daughter of Mankon would follow my example and invest in hope for the younger generations. We owe them the duty.

In terms of our indigenous administrative structures, I have since accession to power in 1959, ensured consolidation and renewal. Conscious of the importance of written documentation, I have encouraged the keeping of written records of all discussions, meetings and decisions in the meetings of all palace institutions. The keeping of minutes is crucial for posterity. To this end, I have appointed to the ranks of decision makers and representatives a new crop of leader with formal and informal education who have the ability to read and write. Where this has not always been possible, I have encouraged my notables to acquire some measure of literacy. When it dawned on me in the early 1990s that most of the deliberations and discussions I had with the various governing institutions and organs in Mankon were not effectively disseminated amongst the wider population of Mankon as they ought to be, and that even policies destined to be diffused to the population ended up after each session of deliberations within the four walls of the palace, I decided to adopt new dimension of effective communication with the people of Mankon. Since then, I have systematically supplemented my communication machinery with the people, hitherto exclusively through the governing institutions organs, with written memoranda directly destined for consumption by the Mankon masses. Consoling enough, the Mankon people are relatively much more literate now than 50 years ago. This innovation has meant that well meaning Mankon citizens are free to put up written memoranda to the Fo and his governing organs, on any issue deemed necessary. It has proved very expedient to be able to communicate with the people in writing, especially at this day and age characterized by accelerated mobility and dispersal of Mankon people throughout the world who remain keen on feeding from and into developments at home.

What I am doing is not earning a salary. I have only a small venture, nothing else. What I am doing for them, I am a full administrator. I organize the village administration, justice, the settlement of peace here and there. Helping their children acquire education and find a foothold in life. I think I am with them, they are with me. We are now aiming for a university. The education I suffered to have when I crossed over to Nigeria is now at the door steps of the children. The same is true for health centres, electricity and other amenities, which are available and the number growing.

In agriculture, I am encouraging others to take it up, at the same time as I am widening the farms. Agriculture reinforces one's sense of self-reliance, and when done scientifically, the increase in crop yields is phenomenal. Simple techniques of soil conservation by planting of cover crops and farming across the slope, wild fire prevention, alternatives to soil and grass burning, manure generation in place of shifting cultivation, the judicious administration of fertilisers, and establishment of demonstration plots have proved revolutionary in our case. So, not only do I supplement my income and provide adequate subsistence for the family, I and the Mankon people who join me on the path of agriculture are able to stand tall against all opportunists seeking to manipulate and manoeuvre over us with empty rhetoric about change. Agriculture makes one dream with their feet firmly on the ground. If you know where your next meal is going to come from, you are not going to sell your soul to ramblers and dissemblers promising everything.

I have also been preoccupied with forestry, planting trees, which we have done as far back as the 1930s when coffee farming was introduced in the region. Initially, the purpose for tree planting was essentially for firewood and building material. The eucalyptus forest plantation was first located in Mankon on the right bank of the river Mezam, and extended from the Ntamulung to Mulang plain. Between 1944 and 1945, the plantation yielded income from the sale of sawn timber, poles, firewood, seeds and seedlings. The forest suffered a setback from an invasion of locusts, which caused considerable damage to the vegetation. Coffee and eucalyptus trees were damaged. When I became Fo Mankon, I continued with forest farming in 1964, on a site along the Bamenda –Mbengwi road called Akfungbe. In 1978, I bought eucalyptus seedlings from the forest nursery in Mendankwe, and subsequently, I nursed more for transplanting. Furthermore, in January 1987, I applied for assistance from the Divisional Delegate of Agriculture for Mezam to supply me with eucalyptus seeds, watering cans, wheelbarrows, pick axes, spades and polythene bags. The Delegate responded positively, enabling me to share some of the seedlings with other interested Mankon farmers. Subsequently, seedlings also came from the Kilum Mountain Forest Project in Oku Subdivision, and from the National Forestry Development Agency, especially after we had a fire disaster and lost much of the forest. Over the years, many Mankon people have emulated my efforts at forestry, planting eucalyptus trees and earning a living there from. In addition, we have pioneered the setting up of a Cameroon Association of Tree Planters for the whole of the North West Region. We are researching and planting different income generating trees, and are currently mapping out the forest to maximise the returns we generate from it, by minimising the planting of exotic trees in favour of the indigenous trees.

In terms of cash and food crops, for long we depended on coffee, but when coffee prices fell, we were forced to convert our coffee farms to the cultivation of other crops. The farms around the palace were then used for planting food crops like bananas, plantains, cocoyams, yams, cassava and maize. We also converted them into orchards where fruit trees such as mangoes, pears, plums, pineapples and guavas were grown. In 1974, I initiated the Asongkah Green Revolution Effort Group. The project started as a self help food sufficiency group and was gradually upgraded into a cooperative society. Initially, only members of the royal family were co-opted as members. I was the president. Later on, membership was extended to include other Mankon farmers.

The main aim of the project was to contribute to the socio-economic development of Mankon through agriculture. Another reason for starting this cooperative was to teach the children of members of the group the importance of agriculture, and by so doing, to increase awareness of the laws of the land in them, thereby ensuring employment and curbing rural exodus. I was also out to encourage, through practice, the adoption and institutionalisation of modern farming techniques amongst the population. Labour in the farm came largely from the royal family, and occasionally from members of the Nte-Afon Young Farmers and similar groups. In 1975, we benefitted from a loan of 2,492,000FCFA from the National Fund for Rural Development (FONADER). This was followed in 1976 by a supply of 10,000 java and Arabica coffee trees by the Department of Agriculture for Bamenda Central Subdivision. What we produced was primarily for subsistence and also for sale. We also tried our hand at pig and poultry farming, but diseases did not permit us to yield as much as we had hoped.

With the collapse of the coffee sector, I switched my attention to oil palm cultivation, which I started in 1975 with a total of surface area of 23 hectares of land at Asongkah, Ala-Bukam and Ala-Mandum. In 1976, I added seven hectares. Seedlings were bought from the now defunct Wum Area Development Authority (WADA) in 1977, and from the Teze Extension and Training Section in 1991. Production of palm oil started in 1985, and by 1990 machines were installed for this purpose. Oil production is usually at its peak in August, with approximately four hundred litres.

I am modernising agriculture increasingly. When I became Fo Mankon in 1959 it was still possible for the various quarters in Mankon to supply free labour to work on the Fon's farms by cleaning, tilling, planting, weeding, harvesting and even transporting the food to the palace. My farms were plotted out and each village had its own portion on which it worked. Each village programmed when to work and they would all come out on specific days for the work. In those days, it was quite understandable why the Mankon people should frown on my intensive personal involvement with agriculture. But things have changed a lot over the past 50 years. Today I am practically responsible for all the labour I want. I hire extra labour to complement what the family is able to give. Even then, I am confronted with the fact that the prospects for labour from the royal family are getting smaller and smaller as children grow and leave the palace for studies, employment and to set up their own homes after marriage. Their mothers are dying out and getting weak. So I try to see how some small mechanical cultivation can be done and leave light work for weeding and harvesting for those of us who work by hand. We still have a big problem. All the roads here in Mankon quarters are those community roads we dug when Foncha was against us and would not allow anything come this way. Our challenge is to improve on the road system.

I do not like to think about political processes. Prefer thinking about the population – I am after schools, I am a man of technical schools, health centres and agro-pastoral projects – an enabling man. I hate to sit idly by, doing nothing, waiting for Father Christmas. I want to see people benefit from where they are. I want them to raise their income. I want Mankon people to develop their abilities, earn an income and have the right to use their money the way they want. That would make them depend less on the whims and caprices of politics and politicians who promise mountains but can't deliver even the barest minimum. Self-reliance is the key to success. It guarantees that your feet shall be firmly on the ground even when you dream.

I have educated my own children and provided opportunities for education of Mankon children and every child in Mankon to the best of my abilities. I am particularly satisfied that since 1961 when I introduced female education, Mankon has not only become a leader in the number of schools providing education for female students, but also the kingdom with the most educated women in the North West. This is an achievement to celebrate, but we must not rest on our laurels as education is just a means to an end.

I thought that in educating the children that might solve some problems of the family, but each child educated has opted for individual pursuits and hardly ever contributed to the wider project. But I am not disappointed. I believe in education. I believe in fighting for opportunity. If I had the means, I'd educate all my children to the point where whoever can make his PhD let him go for it. What education must not become an end in itself. We must always ask ourselves what a degree enables us to realize. The value of the degree will tell the job he had done with it, but he needs to be able to go ahead, seek or create the job. A degree must be actively productive to be relevant. In itself, the degree is nothing. Only by producing something does the degree become a meaningful achievement.

Until you die, you never stop being educated. That is what I tell my children from when they are still very tender. First you should know your brother and know your sister. You should even know who is capable and who is not. Like I learnt when I was made Fo Mankon, your father, your mother, and the wider society spend the best part of their lives educating themselves about who you really are, and what exactly you are capable of. When these things come together, they can say with exactitude whom to count on if they want this or that.

When in 1959 I resisted becoming Fo Mankon, with the king makers and my mothers insisting, it was because they had, together with my father, studied me and reached the conclusion that I was their candidate for Fo. Now, if under that system of education, one of my brothers were, forty to fifty years later, to lay claim to being Fo Mankon, everybody would ask him, 'What are you talking about? If you had ambition to be Fo, why didn't you let us know at the time we enthroned the current Fo?' Even I would add my voice to that of the public and say, 'I could have given you this thing and continued my work.' If you are not a candidate, you should know your successor. There is no magic about it. But the Fo's opinion is final, because he has educated himself the most about his children and their capabilities. The Fo knows his children. The children should know themselves. And when truly they do, the choice of successor is a surprise to no one.

I have not shown a difference in education, between my sons and daughters. It couldn't be otherwise, since I introduced the education of female children in 1961. I see that there is lots of misunderstanding when the children are not well educated because you'll have your problems and then you should be able to discuss and when you discuss intelligently or you argue responsibly there will be give and take. I don't want a division along lines of the educated and the uneducated, which is why I have spared no effect to educate all my children, without exception.

We need to be united, and to stop blaming one another for our problems. When we are together we discuss together we learn from one another and we make efforts to succeed and we are determined to attain our goals. We must have a forum for dialogue. Children must be able to discuss their problems and they should foresee problems and provide for timely solutions. You can't live a life without problems. My children have to work and save money. When somebody is giving you something, giving you money, don't think that it is because he has saved. See it as a sacrifice. He has sacrificed something to give you. But you have some people who, as soon as they have a brother or sister working, start budgeting for them. They want to know how much they earn a month and they budget the expenditure for him. If they know they are earning a hundred thousand they say this goes for school, this goes for this, this is for me, this is for the brother and so on. They are angry when he doesn't spend everything on them – why is he keeping it to himself alone? When it comes to sharing, people want giant share, when it comes to producing they don't want to produce. So we should work hard as long as you live you should be trying to be of value to yourself and the community. It is compulsory for everybody to do it.

Even in politics, people would be less credulous and consequently more united if they were more educated. They would demand greater levels of proof when they are fed stories about this or that person, and would certainly be less gullible when told by self-seeking politicians that chiefs should be kept out of politics. The level of education of the citizens determines the type of politics they should do. People should be able to read newspapers and watch television and listen to radio critically. It is not enough to be in politics only to give food and drinks and to cheer and swallow whatever rhetoric you were fed. It is my hope that once the people are educated they will understand their roles and act their parts well.

Education has made my administration easier. I have re-organised the quarters, creating quarter and area councils, using literate leaders. People are able to address letters and memoranda to me directly, thanks to their ability to read and write, and many are better able to differentiate between falsehood and truth. When I issue a royal act – like the one I did on December 5 2008 banning wake keeping at funerals and forbidding the hiring and firing of guns in the Kingdom of Mankon – I know that many people are going to read and make sense of the reasons for the ban directly, without having to rely on hearsay, which minimises distortions and opportunistic interpretations. Education is a value to cherish and reproduce for the great glory of our people and cultural values, especially these days when the love of money has tended to downgrade human value. Our education must reinforce rather than diminish our humanity and community spirit. It must yield togetherness, not individualism.

I have helped more than 200 children with their schooling here and there. But, I don't need them to be different, they are what they are. My children who think of me, I know them. Those who don't, I know. But what I want of all the children is for them to be together. If you are choristers, I want the choir to be excellent, just like any choir with a good choir master. You my children should know yourselves. Unity and togetherness are key in everything, amongst you my children as amongst the entire Mankon people. In MACUDA everywhere, that's the message I preach – the message of unity and solidarity, as the best guarantee for the development we crave. I preach by example. Even some of our educated and highly placed sons and daughters of Mankon, who distanced themselves from me during the violent politics of mudslinging of the 1990s, those who would not come to the palace anymore, and who lampooned me in the newspapers and in private and public gatherings; even those one, when they have repented and come back to the fold, I have forgiven them.

It is this quest for unity and solidarity that took me touring all the branches of the Mankon Cultural and Development Association (MACUDA) throughout Cameroon. Through with Cameroon, I decided to continue mission in the United States of America, where the biggest Mankon diaspora outside of Cameroon is concentrated. My first visit to the USA was in 2002, while the second took place in October 2007. When I made my maiden visit to the USA in 2002, it was mostly appraise myself with the living conditions and circumstances of my children and the children of Mankon people studying, and living and working in that Country. During that trip in 2002, I also visited the City halls of Worcester, Lowell and Boston, where I told the honourable Mayors, City Managers and City Councillors and Governors that I had come to see where my children and subjects reside, school and work.

During the second visit commencing October 2007, for over three months, I flew the skies and walked the streets of America, meeting sons and daughters of Mankon, Cameroonians and Africans. At Brown University in Connecticut, I gave a lecture on 'How did colonialism either preserve or undermined traditional governance in Africa', and answered questions on various aspects of postcolonial, modern and traditional rule in Cameroon and Africa, including questions on 'How Moslems, Christians and traditional religion coexist peacefully and in Cameroon'. At the Museum of Comparative Zoology, Harvard, I saw several frog species samples; from the smallest type to the hairy frogs collected from Cameroon. At the John F. Kennedy Presidential Library & Museum in Boston, I evoked the memories of the Late President Kennedy and received a thunderous applause and admiration from my audience, when I talked of the Peace Corps Volunteers sent by John F. Kennedy to help in Mankon.

I hope that my actions have opened doors of opportunities for Mankon America. Already, MACUDA have assured me that they are going to invite the Peace Corps Volunteers to MACUDA events at home and abroad. One way to do this is to mobilize and engage all MACUDA branches at home and abroad to connect with present and former Peace Corps Volunteers who have served and are serving in Cameroon. MACUDA branches in Cameroon should organize a reception party for Peace Corps volunteers and their families in Cameroon. They should collect personal contact information, most importantly their email addresses, and keep the Peace Corps abreast with development and other initiatives back home.

When Peace Corps are posted abroad, they are told to bring the world back home with them. It is equally important to stay in touch with that world, since we live in an ever changing world. In this MACUDA can play a key bridging role.

If the enthusiastic reporting on the Internet and in discussion forums by the mostly youthful Mankon population I met, conversed with and addressed all over the USA is anything to go by, then, to quote them, 'the 21st century will forever remain in the annals of history as a century when the Kingdom of Mankon discovered and was discovered by America.' They described my visit to the Commonwealth of Massachusetts, as a traditional ruler from Cameroon in particular, and Africa in general, as unprecedented. I was greeted with much exhilaration, and according to the reports the youth of Mankon shared amongst themselves and with the outside world, my 'eloquence and intelligence echoed from the City halls to the streets of America.' Americans of all walks of life met and exchanged with me, some calling my visit a life time experience and a blessing for them. Mankon, Bamenda, Cameroon and Africa became the talk of the day and the topic for discussion on the streets, at schools and at gatherings. Throughout the most enriching contact tours of the USA, I called on the Cameroonians and Africans I met to connect Americans with Cameroon and Africa, and also to seek to establish sister cities relationships between American cities and cities in Cameroon and Africa. In this regard, a fruit of my 2002 visit was the establishment of a sister city accord between Lowell and Bamenda.

I have seen the value of people living together, discussing and learning from one another, and getting assistance from one another. Even if you don't need material assistance, in the general discussion I learn something from you, you have assisted me. In other words what you are doing will never be permanently yours, you will pass it over. If you will build a house you will leave it to the children. If you have a raffia bush it will go to the children. The fact that nobody lives forever should be motivation enough for us to think of others. Even the millionaire, the money in the bank is not his own. The sooner we all realize that we come into life only to build the society and pass over, the better we would tax ourselves enough to leave our marks in the sands of time, on the road we have trailed. The task of building a prosperous Mankon for our children and generations to come is much too important for us to approach in dispersed ranks. I pray that each generation should create a peaceful atmosphere. When they pass away they leave it to the other generation. They will take their assets and the liabilities and that is a good liability.

Earlier, I mentioned the importance of land and our status as landlord if we are to remain relevant as a collectivity and a cultural community. Our land management is currently not the best. It has tended to create more landless citizens. The love for money and riches by selling land has not been good for the population. By so doing, they have been exchanging gold for nickel instead of developing it for themselves. Our future as a community is tightly linked to how successful we manage the land at our disposal as a scarce resource, which is why on September 30 2003, I signed a royal act regulating the sale of land in the Kingdom of Mankon.

My call for judicious land management must not be mistaken for a call for Mankon people to be hostile towards strangers. My father started the policy of integrating people from elsewhere into Mankon. He had seen the need for unifying people, and I think anybody of good behaviour could benefit from this largesse and his grand children could become Mankon and practice the culture. The world now is one, whether one is black or white. All have a place in Mankon, and whoever plays his part well will achieve his objectives. In July 2008, I signed a related royal act, regulating building construction, provision and maintenance of infrastructure within the Kingdom of Mankon, in tune with my ambition for aesthetic value, need and importance on a well planned and enviable modern Mankon.

Opening up to other cultures and people does not imply that Mankon should neglect its own culture. Mankon culture must be maintained and not exchanged for foreign cultures. Rather, our culture should integrate other ways of seeing and doing that we find positive in others. It is the task of the young and upcoming generations to hold and enrich our culture through encounters with others.

For my part, I have done what I could to maintain our culture while simultaneously opening up to other influences. I have seen it as my duty and the duty of all Mankon people to protect and promote the cultural values that have characterised us as a community for centuries. It was with this in mind that I dedicated efforts and resources towards making the Mankon Museum a reality. So, if I were to assess myself, I would say one of my greatest achievements has been the renovation of the Museum in the palace, which today brings Mankon cultural heritage home to sons and daughters of Mankon, and also to tourists. Over the years, I have been concerned about the safety of these antiquities, constantly threatened by fire, termites and theft.

In the early 1960s during the Independence cerebrations of Cameroon, the Minister of Education and Culture at the time and his cultural adviser Reverend Englebert Mveng, took along with them for display in America some of our antiquities. This was done rather clandestinely, as it later dawned on me. While there, they did not treat the dancers well and the dancers came back abandoning the instruments. The Mankon Traditional Council and the dancers complained about the matter to the United Nations Visiting Mission but all attempts to recover the antiquities failed. We learnt that the Cameroon Ambassador in the USA did not know about the Minister's plan of the cultural display. The Mankon Traditional Council tried to hold the government responsible but the government said it was a private arrangement between the two people, Le Gunsu and Reverend Englebert Mveng, and they died without paying for the antiquities.

In the 1980s, the Cameroon government made tourism a priority. The Mankon people deemed it necessary to construct a modern museum in order to secure the antiquity for posterity. To realise this objective, I appealed for financial and technical assistance. I wrote letters to various possible funders, and also to the Ministry of Tourism. Eventually, a positive response came from the Italian NGO Centro Oreintamento Educativa (COE), with headquarters in Barzio, Italy. The assistance for the museum came when the Italian Ministry of Foreign Affairs opted to give economic and technical support to five small museums in Cameroon for a period of one year. The president of COE, Carls Airoldi, resident in Milan, wrote me a letter on December 4, 2000, bearing the good news. We signed an agreement on June 22 2001, according to the terms of which COE was to assist in the conservation and restoration of the artistic and cultural heritage of the Kingdom, in training the guardship of the cultural property, and develop, improve and equip the museum. Further financial contribution came from the Mankon people.

The Mankon Museum, constructed in conformity with the standards of the International Council of Museums, took five years to complete, and was inaugurated on January 28 2006, complete with a 255 page catalogue – *Mankon: Art, Heritage and Culture from the Mankon Kingdom* – compiled and published in 2005 by Jean-Paul Notué and Bianca Triaca.

I am grateful for this collaboration on the cultural heritage of Mankon, just as I am grateful to all those anthropologists, historians and others who have never relented in their documentation of ways and encounters with others. Amongst these, I am particularly thankful to Jean-Pierre Warnier, a French anthropologist and historian who has written extensively on various aspects of Mankon since the 1970s, and who has always sent copies of his writings to the palace, where he is known as *Sangto'* – the Palace Courtyard – a title I gave in 1974 in recognition of his achievements for Mankon. My acknowledgement also goes to *Mafo Sangto'* Jacqueline Leroy, his wife at the time, for her two detailed books and a number of articles on the Mankon language. It is pleasing to know that they have remained committed and active in their study of and interaction with Mankon, inspiring our own scholars to rise to the challenge of recording the happenings and realities of our society.

Historians like Thaddeus Achu Anye and Nicodemus Fru Awasom have demonstrated the importance of having Mankon perspectives on Mankon history. The best recognition I can hope for in appreciation for the efforts I have made to promote education in Mankon, is for the young and upcoming generations to borrow from the example of all these anthropologists and historians and ensure that our culture and experiences are well documented. For, it is only in documenting and preserving our past that we are best able to organise the present in the interest of the future.

The Mankon Museum is testimony to the fact that the best way of consolidating our traditions is to make them modern, and that our modernity only makes sense to the extent that it is firmly grounded in our traditions. In many ways I feel my life encapsulates this negotiation and reconciliation of continuity and change. I am what my father was not, but I clearly couldn't have been without what my father was. I have contributed my modest best in giving Mankon a sense of direction and meaning within our ever changing and ever familiar landscape. It is up to our young and upcoming generations to take the baton and excel in honour of Mankon, Cameroon and Africa.

8

My Life in Photos

Fo Ndefru III

Mafo Angwafo III

Young Prince

Fo Mankon

Fo Angwafo III S.A.N of Mankon

Fo Angwafo III S.A.N of Mankon

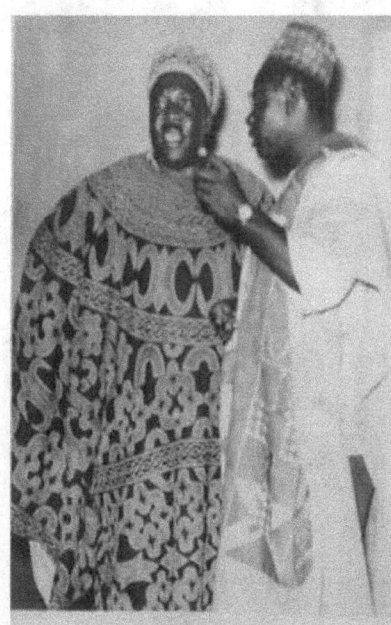

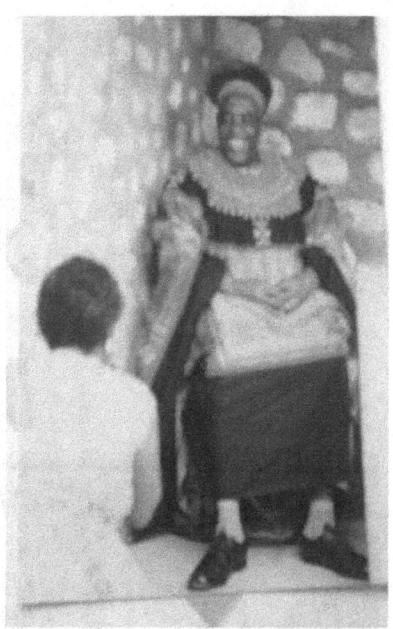

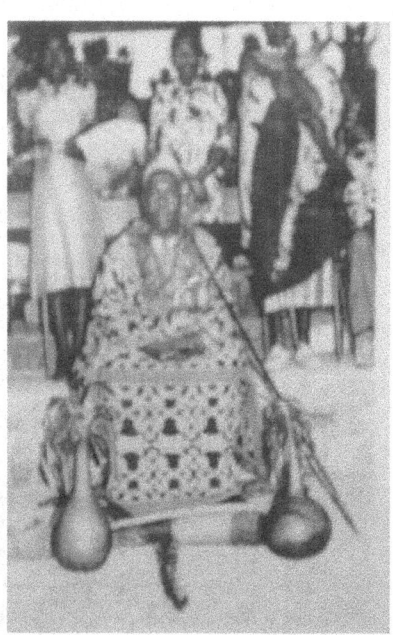

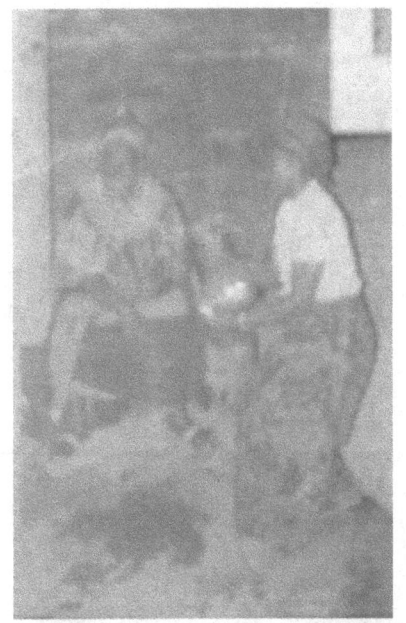

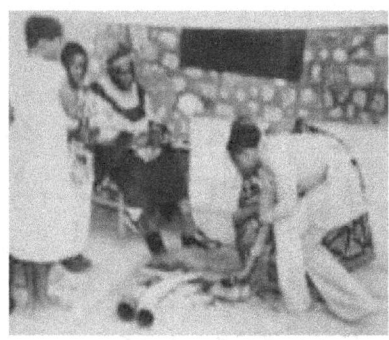

MaFo

Fo and Politics

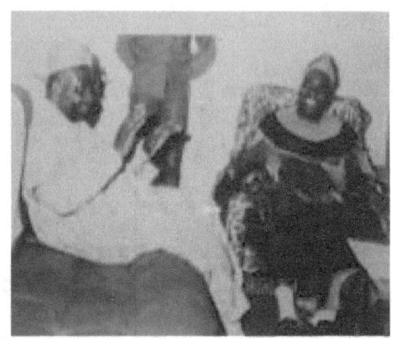

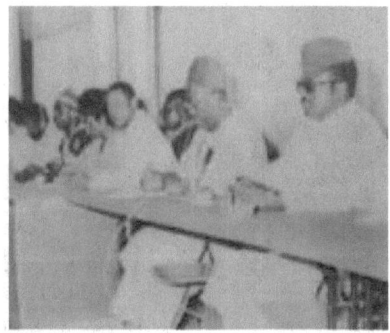

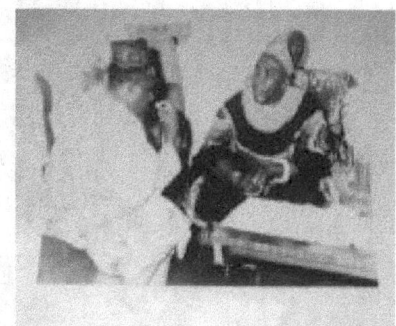

Abengafo

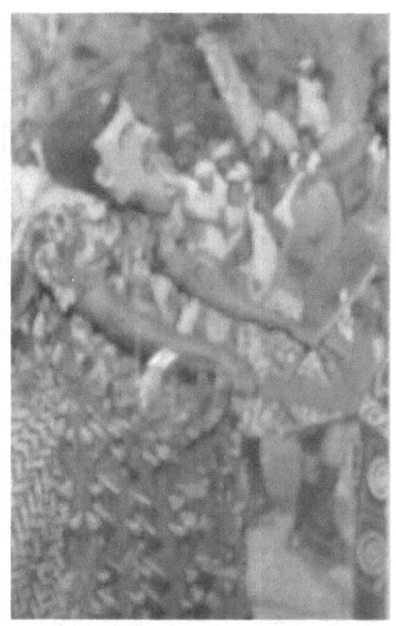

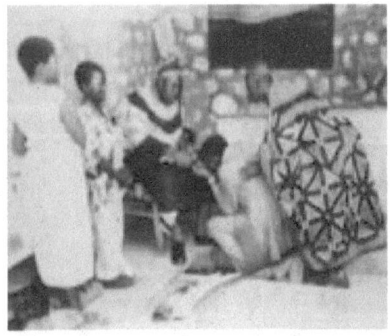

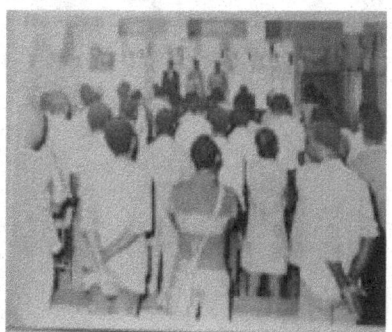

Awards

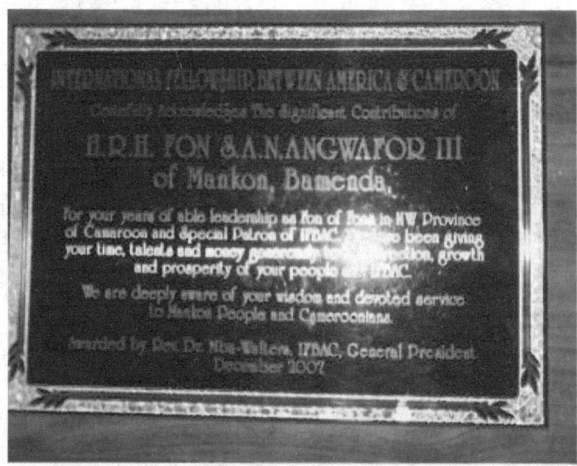

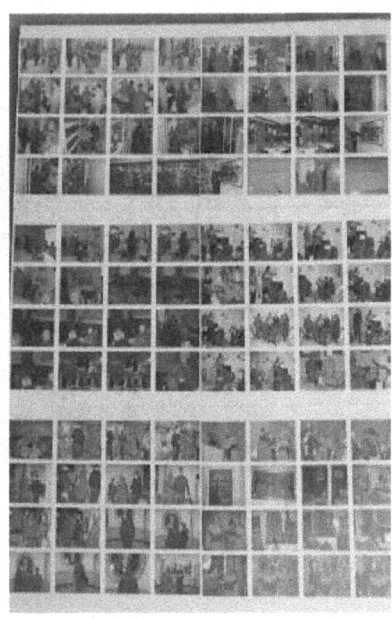

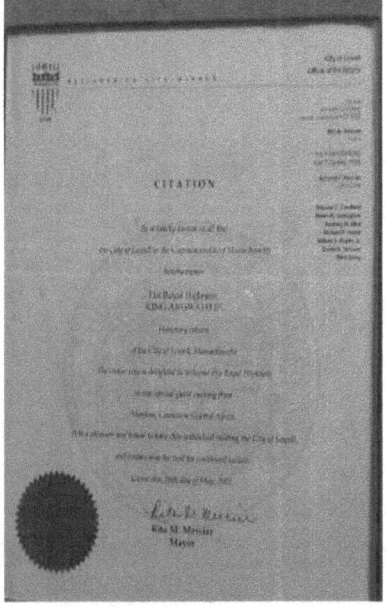

www.ingramcontent.com/pod-product-compliance
Lightning Source LLC
Chambersburg PA
CBHW011744290426
44113CB00017BA/2652